Remembered Forever

Our family's devastating story
of domestic abuse and murder

LUKE AND RYAN HART

SEVEN DIALS

Originally published in Great Britain in 2018
as *Operation Lighthouse*
This revised and updated edition published
in Great Britain in 2019 by Seven Dials
an imprint of The Orion Publishing Group Ltd
Carmelite House, 50 Victoria Embankment
London EC4Y 0DZ

An Hachette UK Company

1 3 5 7 9 10 8 6 4 2

A CIP catalogue record for this book is
available from the British Library.

ISBN (Mass market paperback) 978 1 8418 8340 3
ISBN (eBook) 978 1 8418 8341 0

Typeset by Input Data Services Ltd, Somerset

Printed and bound in Great Britain by Clays Ltd, Elcograf S.p.A.

www.orionbooks.co.uk

For Mum and Charlotte.

Through our words and actions, may you live for ever.

CONTENTS

'All that is necessary for the triumph of evil is that good men do nothing.'

Edmund Burke

FOREWORD

Remembered Forever is a courageous account of domestic abuse and the devastating impact it has on families. Luke and Ryan Hart write powerfully about how the emotional abuse in their family was hidden and unnoticed for decades, resulting in the tragic murders of their mother, Claire, and sister, Charlotte.

We all have a responsibility to ensure that the abuse thousands of women endure is not normalised or tolerated, and that victims feel empowered to seek the help they need. In this horrific story, the whole family were terrorised and unable to speak out. In the words of the great Angela Davis, 'I'm no longer accepting the things I cannot change, I'm changing the things I cannot accept', and it is with this boldness that Luke and Ryan have used their own experience of domestic abuse to help others. They share their story so honestly because they, like me, believe that together we can change society.

Jeremy Corbyn MP

PREFACE

We decided to write this book two years after our mother, Claire, and sister, Charlotte, were murdered by our father. This book details our experiences growing up and our first tentative steps overcoming the tragedies of our lives.

This book was initially written by Luke for Ryan. It was intended to communicate pain too raw and unyielding for us to address in person, too deep and enduring to address in the shortness of spoken conversation.

It grew into a collaborative conversation between the two of us. It allowed us to begin communicating side by side, with the strength of the other always present. We were able to communicate in our own time, at our own speed and in a way that gave us the space we needed to reflect. We could face the emotions alone and when we felt strong enough to bear them.

Now, having come to accept the tragedy of the murders, this book has transformed into the next stage of our journey. We felt the pressing need to challenge the pervasive beliefs which facilitate domestic abuse. We realised that we had to talk about what had happened to our family or we risked condemning other victims with our silence.

Initially, we did not know how we could help – all we had was our story. However, as we shared our experiences, many individuals reached out to us to let us know the impact it had on them. We realised the power of stories to connect our lives, to weave together the fabric of our concerns and compassion, and to help others realise that domestic abuse was not their own personal problem, but a shared experience that many women and children suffer. In some cases, we were told that our story had not only opened others' eyes to domestic abuse but had quite possibly saved their lives.

The following is one particularly inspiring message (we have removed details and names for anonymity):

I wanted to take the time to personally thank you for your involvement in the conference. I was invited by one of my colleagues as a result of my own experience, and predominantly to be given the opportunity to hear your story.

I was going through a difficult time in my relationship last year, my colleague took me to one side and asked if she could carry out a DASH [domestic abuse, stalking and honour-based violence] assessment. She told me that a lot of what I had been talking about sounded very familiar. The reason it sounded familiar was because she had heard your story.

When I saw you on the stage describing your experiences growing up, I could see my children in 20 years' time. Everything you said sounded like you were describing our lives.

To cut a very long story short, as a result of the DASH assessment and subsequent MARAC [multi-agency risk assessment conference] referral, the police became very concerned and put a number of measures in place before I left him. This was all done without his knowledge and I was able to leave (although incredibly frightened), with the peace of mind that I was being protected.

What I am trying to say is thank you both. Thank you for potentially saving the life of myself and my children. Because you chose to speak out, someone became concerned about my situation. Had you not agreed to speak at that conference, her suspicions would not have been raised and my situation may have been an entirely different one.

The whole conference had a huge impact on me and it is something that has not left me. I still feel so numb to think that, if things had been different, my children could have been delivering a very similar speech in years to come.

Stories like these are not our reward for speaking up; they demonstrate that we have a responsibility to tell our story. Therefore, what started as an intimate discussion between the two of us has grown into a wider public dialogue.

We recognised that we needed to highlight how belief systems are responsible for gender violence, not emotion; men, not women. It is society's collective responsibility to actively challenge these damaging beliefs every single day and in every encounter. As we have learned, there is no clearer revelation of societal sexism than the gendered nature of domestic abuse and the conflicting way in which it is then reported.

We decided to write about our lives to allow others to see behind the veil of abuse and draw parallels to their own relationships. On a macro scale, this book addresses the core moral issues which perpetuate abuse in our society by exploring the damaging societal beliefs and stereotypes that we encountered. On a micro scale, we do our best to highlight the daily structural disadvantages that abused women suffer through the eyes of two young men who lived under a brutal patriarch.

Writing was beneficial for both of us as it helped us regain control of the narrative of our lives, tearing ownership away from the murder note our father had left behind. Our father had spent his life contorting our perception of reality. Our freedom has come from taking control of our perspective. Writing installed us as the creators of our lives, a position we had never before occupied. Finding the words for our experiences helped us to unwind everything deep inside. Now we can separate the good from the bad and the joy from the pain and begin to rebuild ourselves.

Before beginning our story, we believe it is key to paint an accurate picture, using facts, of domestic abuse.

Firstly, abusers are far too prevalent to be the anomalous monsters they are often represented as, given that one in four women will suffer domestic abuse in their lifetime in the UK.[1] The sheer number of domestic abuse victims suggests that domestic abuse is not merely the result of intimate partners who cannot control their anger.[2] In fact, 'overall [men who murdered their female partners] were more likely than [men who murdered men] to get on in prison and to be defined as "model prisoners"'.[3] These men have no problems following rules or restraining their instincts in male-dominated environments. These men defer to hierarchy and power structures (in fact they worship power, as we shall see); however, they can be brutal towards those who they consider to be beneath them.

In particular, these men 'specialised in violence against women'. In a study on those convicted of femicide, of those men who had previous histories of physical violence, the usual victim was a woman. The inevitable conclusion is that 'it is men's orientations to and assumptions about the appropriate behaviour of women, their sense of entitlement over women, and the need to uphold their own moral universe that led to the murder of the vast majority of woman partners'.[4]

The particular circumstances of male violence show this to be the case, where 90 per cent of non-domestic homicides are male victims, but 70 per cent of domestic homicides are female victims.[5] Men choose to murder other men in public, often strangers, but women in private, 'their women'.

Given the prevalence of abuse, we must conclude that abusers are common products of masculine culture, not anomalies within it. These men strongly believe in gender stereotypes and hold their partners rigidly accountable to these ideals. 'Abusive husbands don't necessarily have bad views towards women, just their own.'[6] They worship the idea of a submissive wife and they punish their real wife who does not meet their expectations. Compared to non-abusive men, 'abusers were significantly less able to empathise with partners and showed far less positive regard for them, and while abusive men did not score any differently than non-abusive men on tests that assess attitudes towards women in general, they consistently communicate more negative beliefs about their partners'.[7]

The primary factor responsible for domestic abuse is gender, not a lack of emotional control as is often blamed. Many studies have shown that men who believed they were drinking alcoholic drinks at a party, when in fact there had been no alcohol at all in their drinks, became more aggressive than those who knew they were not consuming alcohol. In one study, individuals who falsely believed they had drunk alcohol administered higher levels of electric shocks to individuals who gave the wrong answers to tests. These results suggest that individuals use alcohol as an excuse to act out.[8] Alcohol is not the only excuse presented for domestic abuse, but all excuses follow the same pattern: those who believe their excuse is valid are more likely to abuse.

The deadly consequence of the masculine desire for power and control over intimate partners, combined with the extensive list of purported excuses, is that 50 per cent of all female victims of homicide aged sixteen and over are killed by partners or ex-partners. In contrast, the figure is only 3 per cent for male victims of homicide aged sixteen and over. It would appear that, despite the specious saying, women do not need men to protect them from the outside world. In fact, the home is the most dangerous place for women: around 75 per cent of female victims of homicide were killed at home, as opposed to 38 per cent of male homicides. In addition, the majority of victims aged under sixteen years were killed by a parent or step-parent.[9] All of this shows that women and children are specifically targeted, in the home, and often by those men who are supposed to love them.

Faced with this reality, domestic abuse cannot be passed off as harmless, personal business. Domestic homicides, the most objective measure of domestic abuse, are a large contributor to overall national homicides, accounting for approximately 35 per cent of all murders in England and Wales.[10]

Why, then, is our society so poorly equipped to identify abusers? Why are we always so surprised when domestic homicides occur? Unfortunately, abusers blend into our culture; normality is their cloak of invisibility. Abusers can comfortably carry out abusive behaviours under the veil of traditional romanticism towards partners or patriarchal paternalism towards their families without anyone batting an eyelid.

Even abusive men believe their abusive behaviours are romantic or protective. As discussed, domestic abuse occurs when the abuser believes it is an entitlement, acceptable or justified, and they therefore believe 'real' abuse is what someone else does. They don't believe they are abusers themselves because they believe they always had an excuse for their behaviour; they believe their victim 'deserved it'. Many people do not recognise themselves as abusers or victims because they may view their experiences as family conflicts that have got out of control.[11]

Abuse is also often portrayed as if it were an internal struggle against 'mental illness', or anger, within the perpetrator that spills out upon the family. However, this is not the case. Why do these men behave themselves in society, even to the point of appearing to be 'good men', yet save up their abuse for their family? In most cases, abusers are quite capable of exercising control over themselves, but choose not to do so for various reasons.[12] A key point to understand is that the purpose of abuse is to keep the victims, and sometimes the entire family, subordinate to the abusers. Abusers always have limits that they never cross and they always have carefully calculated goals when they appear to 'lose it'. If abusers break things in a momentary 'loss of control', it is only victims' possessions, never their own, for example. Their moral universe tells them they are allowed to behave like this towards their family, but not their bosses or the neighbours.

If abuse was due to 'mental illness', or poverty, or difficult childhoods, then why is domestic homicide perpetrated predominantly by men towards women? Why do women not kill men for these same reasons? The reason is that it does not matter how traumatised or 'mentally ill' someone is, they will not hurt another person unless they believe it is OK to do so.

Belief systems are the primary reason that men commit domestic abuse; their actions and emotions flow from their beliefs. Abuse is based entirely around controlling victims – women and children – because of male patriarchal entitlement; the belief that men should be in charge, at all costs. Often, what are asserted as causes are actually post-rationalised excuses. These excuses are generated by men who want to abuse their partners for not living up to their idealised but highly restrictive view of femininity, and abusers will sometimes intentionally harm their children to distress their partners further.

The most common misunderstanding we have encountered around domestic abuse is the failure to consider the innumerable, sometimes small, sometimes large, but accumulating tensions that cause victims to behave the way they do. A lack of understanding of victims, due to their silence, either enforced during their lives or through the ultimate act of control of taking their lives, normally manifests in a question, such as: 'Why do victims of domestic abuse put up with it?'

To answer this, it is necessary to focus on the normalisation of domestic abuse. Abuse often occurs for long periods of time, sometimes explicitly acknowledged by others and not challenged or implicitly understood and accepted by others. External condoning of the abuse leads the victims to consider their experiences normal.[13] In fact, in a study of victims of attempted domestic abuse-related homicide, only half of the participants recognised that their perpetrator was capable of killing them.[14]

Many abusers will further disarm victims with confusion by creating the conditions of abuse while forming a position for themselves as a 'saviour'. Our father did this by working as little as possible, wasting what little money we had and then using poverty as an eternal justification to control our finances, while at the same time claiming he was 'volunteering his time to run our bank accounts and manage all the family finances'. In our case, the evidence of abuse was not what our father explicitly did to us, through bruises and broken limbs, but what we could never do: it wasn't the visible traces, but the invisible lives we lost and the opportunities that couldn't be realised.

How do abusers get their victims to such a point of powerlessness? The abusers may have isolated their victims during the initial stages of their relationships. This is often achieved by blinding the victims to the abusers' manipulative tactics through love-bombing, where the abusers will weaponise love to form dependency in their victims. The abusers may then try to spend as much time as possible with their victims so that family and friends drift away and their victims gradually become isolated. The victims' isolation may only become visible once the abusers no longer feel the need to deploy this 'love' any longer, having already gained control. For children growing up under abuse, they understand these conditions to be normal because it is all they have ever known. It is very easy indeed for an abuser to control the perspectives of children who are still learning right and wrong.

The most dangerous abusers will present a different persona to the outside world. After all, they only want control of their intimate partners, they do not spray abuse in all directions (as the defunct stereotype of a 'mentally ill' man who suffers from 'emotional loss of control' would suggest). This two-sidedness to abusers means the victims will not only hear that their experiences are normal from their abusers, but also from everyone else looking in.

To overcome the powerlessness caused by abuse and the mental anguish associated with it, victims must often recalibrate their perspectives so that they do not descend into unbearable despair: often called gaining 'control in the context of no control'. Where victims have no physical control of their external situations, they often exercise psychological or emotional control over themselves. They have to find a way to function each day; victims must make life more bearable by minimising their distress, which often means disregarding the abuse and focusing on other aspects of their lives as much as possible. For this reason, victims of abuse may, in fact, be incredibly successful in certain areas of their life. They are likely to be projecting themselves away from the abuse and trying to create an identity and independence in response to the abusers' repression.

Victims must continually balance between short-term survival strategies and long-term escape strategies. Short-term survival requires a level of emotional stability that sacrifices acknowledging the truly terrifying nature of their existence. To accept the terrifying reality would plunge them into crippling fear and they would lose their ability to function daily.

Victims of abuse learn strategies to reduce the abuse they suffer. Primarily, they find ways to reduce conflict, such as appearing less threatening, quieter and more conforming. Only once they find enough space for survival can they begin to plan for escape. However, abusers have an instinct for constricting their victims each time victims attempt to create more space for themselves. Abusers sense the increasing independence and resolve of their victims and ratchet up the abuse each time the victims try to minimise it. If you consider the unreasonableness of abusers and their controlling and manipulative natures, you begin to realise that ordinary conflict resolution strategies only increase the abuse suffered by victims. Abusers cannot be compromised with, they demand absolute control. This is why the actions of victims may seem counterintuitive from an outside perspective, but are highly rational within the context of abuse. Victims become the experts of negotiating the impossible idiosyncrasies of their abusers.

Abusers are not interested in resolving conflict because their goal is to create ever-escalating conflict until they gain control of their victims through their total submission. Any apparent attempts by abusers to resolve conflict are disingenuous and manipulative in nature. These attempts are often aimed at disarming victims and lowering their level of awareness to facilitate the encroachment of more control. The abusers' ultimate goal is to get inside their victims' heads.

By the time victims realise the nature of their abusers, the abusers may have managed to control the victims' resources or the victims may have dependants whom they cannot leave behind. Often, abusers force their partners out of work, leaving victims dependent upon their abusers for subsistence.

Once victims reach this state, why do they not scream their suffering at the top of their voices? Well, for some their perception is so distorted and they are so confused that they don't realise how much they are being controlled. For many, there simply is no outlet; victims speak but there is no one left to listen because they are so isolated. Inevitably, victims learn reticence. Our society is still not good at talking about abuse, so victims eventually begin to doubt the authenticity of their experiences and the validity of their claims against injustice.

Abusers engender fear in their victims to reduce their space for action, to make them fear doing anything at all, except the narrow existence the abusers allow. It is often said that where there is fear there is no consent. The reality is that victims often have very little choice regarding their situations. This is the abusers' goal: to entrap the victims, economically, emotionally, psychologically and socially.

Abusers are often able to control their victims even when they have separated because their levers of control extend across the victims' entire lives: they do not require proximity or a persisting relationship. The abusers' intimate knowledge of the victims allows them to exploit their victims' habits, routines and vulnerabilities. Therefore, the public's interrogative focus should not be on the victims' actions, who have been imprisoned within their own lives. 'Why doesn't she leave her abuser?' is a strange question considering 75 per cent of women killed by partners are killed after they leave. Surely we should be asking: 'Why don't men let their partners leave?' and 'Why do men stalk, harass and abuse, even when relationships are over?'

Men control their intimate partners using a strategy referred to as coercive control. Coercive control is defined by the Home Office as, 'behaviour [that] does not relate to a single incident, it is a purposeful pattern of incidents that occur over time in order for one individual to exert power, control or coercion over another'. Controlling behaviour specifically is 'a range of acts designed to make a person subordinate and/or dependent by isolating them from sources of support, exploiting their resources and capacities for personal gain, depriving them of the means needed for independence, resistance and escape and regulating their everyday behaviour'. Coercive behaviour is 'an act or a pattern of acts of assault, threats, humiliation and intimidation or other abuse that is used to harm, punish, or frighten their victim'.[15]

It is important to understand that coercive control is not simply a catalogue of misdemeanours committed by an abuser. Many understand domestic abuse to only be about bruises or broken bones. 'What did he do to you?' is the immediate question. However, that understands only one paradigm of abuse. It ignores the types of abuse that are persistent, every minute of every day, and designed to grind you down until you are nothing. Coercive control is the aggregation of events, often not even physical, which individually might not be a heinous crime, but like death, erode us down slowly and persistently with time. Each abuse creates an atmosphere of fear for the victims, which is much greater than the sum of its parts and persists after the 'abuse stops'. Domestic abuse must be evaluated based not on what was done by the abusers but on what was feared by the victims. Coercive control is murder with a million pin pricks over many years; no one thinks much of each prick but the victims fear something serious will happen, they just don't know when.

Our father had not been explicitly violent towards us but he turned our home into an economic, emotional and psychological prison. When we found out about the killings, since we did not understand coercive control, it seemed that our father's murders of Mum and Charlotte had come out of nowhere. We had understood domestic abuse to be about violence, but the violence came all at once. However, it was only when we understood domestic abuse to be about power and control, and when we understood murder as the ultimate act of control, that we were able to see the truth of our experiences. Suddenly, we could see that our father's actions followed a trend of increasing control that had been developing our entire lives.

Coercive control is a liberty crime, of the order of kidnapping or hostage-taking. When we understand this, the behaviours of victims makes sense in the context of the socio-economic prison they are constrained within. Given their situation, victims often make the best decisions they can. It is onlookers who are ignorant and fail to see the prison. Even if onlookers might happen to notice a bar or two and see the victims' submissive demeanour, they often fail to see the full enclosure.

Given that abusers often leverage structural disadvantages to entrap victims, it is easier for men to coercively control women by constructing such socio-economic prisons than vice versa because men are 'simply enforcing gender stereotypes'. However, to many men, women's gender stereotypes are of unpaid domestic slaves under male domination, making male domination of women socially condoned. Few concerns are raised by onlookers when women are dominated in their private lives.

In coercive control, the entire goal of abusers is to force their victims to stay under their domination. Our father's behaviour made us all, but particularly our mother, a socio-economic hostage; slave to his masculine insecurity. As we have learned, we must not treat 'domestic' as a mitigating factor in abuse, but as a magnification factor. If abusers know their victims' fears, habits, travel patterns, work and friends and family, abusers can leverage this information to deprive liberty. Strangers could never cause such a level of intimate devastation.

It should now be clear that those who suggest domestic abuse and domestic homicide can be reduced to individual mental illness and resolved by psychiatrists are guilty of attempting to narrow abuse down to the level of the individual, rather than address the key structural forces responsible for pervasive domestic abuse. In fact, if we reflect on most psychological problems we often find a sociological cause that necessitates a political solution. 'Mental illness' is one of many covers abusers use to avoid responsibility for their actions. Domestic abuse is treated as isolated incidents so that women feel it is their own fault, rather than due to endemic male violence and entitlement. This tactic of atomising abuse makes it difficult for victims to come together and demand change in society. But victims of abuse are not responsible for their situations. We all are. Domestic abuse is not caused by isolated, emotional incidents but by persistent, gendered evil on a societal level.

We hope that our story can demonstrate that evil is very close to home. If we do not tackle the family as the source of gender violence, all of our efforts will only be remediating the outcome of the problem. Male paternalism towards women and children is analogous to philanthropy as it exploits a socio-economic system (the patriarchy) rigged in men's collective favour and then forces dependence based on men's goodwill, which can be removed at any time. Women and children do not need protection or support from men, they need liberty and freedom from men's abuse. It is not insignificant that our father often referred to us only by our patriarchal relevance: 'Woman', 'Boy', 'Girl'. We did not have identities separated from our subordination to him.

Overcoming domestic abuse requires expecting more from the men around us. The justifications proposed and accepted for male abuse, violence and murder are an insult to every good man. When men, like our father, commit familicide there is always a dash in the media to find out the man's life story and an army of apologists rush in to lament for the poor man who felt he had no option but to kill his family. We mustn't make martyrs out of murderers, especially not those supporting a masculinity we need to dispose of. It is not feminists who hate men, it is these apologists who lower men to simple emotional automatons, who have so little respect for men as to expect nothing else from us.

In order to uproot abuse from families, we need to address the way in which the media inhibits action and panders to populist views rather than driving beneficial change. When the media fails to call out domestic abuse as a societal pattern of male violence against women and children, but instead reports disconnected incidents, they isolate victims in death as the abusers did in the victims' lives. It is key to call out domestic abuse for what it is because the true damage of growing up with domestic abuse is being taught that it is normal.

Normalisation of abuse forces victims to internalise the abuse rather than resist it. Lazy use of language or societal silence on the true causes of domestic abuse lead to the incorrect allocation of moral focus. It dismisses victims' suffering as isolated mental illness and excuses abusers' actions. It appears that our society does not wish to see that sexism lies at the heart of abuse, because this would hold us all to account to change.

Our society fails to relate to victims because we are uncomfortable with tragedy exposing our failings as bystanders. The tragedies of others also reveal to us the innumerable similar instances where, with only a slight displacement of luck, our lives could have equally imploded. We do not want to consider our own fragility so we try to distance ourselves from victims, to blame them, to feel that they deserved it and we didn't. As bystanders, our responsibility is to always ensure that we see the story from the perspective of the victims, not the perpetrators.

Yet, our murdering father was eulogised in the press, which chose his perspective. We were forced to read of our father's 'suicide note' rather than the 'murder note' that it was to our mother and sister. We were forced to read of passers-by who lauded our father, where no questions were asked to understand our mother and sister. We were forced to read a story that began when we escaped our father and finished when he killed our mother and sister. But our story began twenty-five years earlier. It is key we attempt to understand victims because, if we want to improve the world, we need to understand those it is failing.

Beyond the media, we all have a responsibility to talk about domestic abuse. Evil is bred in stagnant, societal silence and it grows from the insidious and persistent toleration of small-scale abusive actions. In fact, often coercive control consists entirely in the accumulation of subtler abuse, but aggregated over years this abuse is devastating. Therefore, to disrupt male violence early, we must all be braver in condemning everyday male control and abuse that reinforces masculine dominance belief systems which are responsible for male abuse of women and children.

A key point we feel that needs addressing, and a point that frequently comes up when we talk about abuse, is that men can suffer from domestic abuse too. We couldn't agree more. While many of the messages we have received have been from women, those that we received from men were in fact talking about the abuse they suffered from their fathers. The fear in their recollections was evident.

Men often suffer the worst abuse from other men. Research shows that abuse by men is qualitatively different to abuse by women: 70 per cent of female victims in one study were 'very frightened' in response to intimate partner violence from their partners, but 85 per cent of male victims cited 'no fear'.[16] This is due to the fact that men and women are generally violent for different reasons; men are violent to control and kill, and almost all women who kill their partners do so in self-defence against abusive partners or to escape.[17] An interesting story illustrates this. In the US, the first women's shelters were introduced in the mid-1970s. In 1976, male and female partners were statistically almost equally likely to be killed. These shelters then allowed women to escape abusive husbands but, rather than reducing the number of women killed by men, it has had mostly the opposite effect, causing the number of husbands killed by wives to reduce. By 2004, the number of domestic homicides had reduced by 70 per cent for men killed by women but only 20 per cent for women killed by men.[18] The presence of shelters enabled women to escape from their abuser instead of, in some cases, resorting to murder, yet the abusive men found another victim. Men often are the instigators of serious violence; women are often reacting to the conflict that men create.

It is important to acknowledge that addressing male violence is in men's interests too. A 2013 global study on homicide by the United Nations Office on Drugs and Crime found that males accounted for 96 per cent of all homicide perpetrators worldwide and 75 per cent of the victims were male.[19] Masculinity, and its desire for dominance, is a key factor responsible for male violence: towards other men, women and children, and themselves. Men abuse and are violent to one another to fight for their position of dominance, and men abuse and are violent to women and children to remind them that they are dominated. Since male violence is rooted in our masculine beliefs, all men have a role to play in reducing male violence by joining the conversation to sculpt the masculine value system towards something more harmonious and fundamentally worthwhile.

So, if men are struggling so much within the constructs

of our gender, why are some defending it so heavily? The reason is simple: because misogynistic masculinity is a great place to hide for the loveless and those incapable of love. It offers those men incapable of, or unwilling to, love an alternative: power and control. Men's rights groups who claim they are supporting men with their anti-feminist backlash are misguided or disingenuous. Their goal is to attack equality in all its forms; they desire the maintenance of all power structures held over others. They are only defending masculinity, not men.

The level of self-pity and perceived victimisation of misogynistic men is ironic as it plays contrary to the apparent stereotype of male stoicism demanded by those very same chauvinists. In an attempt to defend their perceived masculinity, they demonstrate exactly the kind of weakness they despise. These men are so delicately sensitive and easily offended that it would be pitiful if it was not veiled in an aggressive rage.

Abusers focus on their feelings and your behaviours. Good men focus on your feelings and their behaviours. When witnessing these childish outbursts we must remember that, to those who are accustomed to privilege, equality feels like oppression. They are not accustomed to seeing life through the eyes of others.

Within this context of male domination, it is clear that domestic abuse is not about violence, but control. Violence is simply one means of enforcing control. But despite the control these men have, they are miserable. These men own their families but they are not a part of them. They control their partners but cannot love them. They have material wealth but emotional emptiness. These men have become alienated from themselves.

Masculine culture necessitates men to believe that we are godlike, which makes us somewhat hostile to criticism. It is due to the Faustian bargain we made: we sacrificed worthwhile emotional experiences or connection, but we demanded power in return.

If anyone on the outside of the cult raises concerns about masculine culture, it closes ranks and unites against a common enemy. Masculinity is relational; it is constructed in relation to and against an Other, which it perceives to be below it (for example: femininity). If we could all be who we wanted to be, then there would be no distinct Other: there would be no prize for the masculine sacrifice.

If anyone on the inside of the cult raises concerns, masculine dogma shames its members into conformity or forces them to run the gauntlet to escape. It uses taunts, threats and violence to discourage independent thinking and to enforce its worship of hierarchy.

Men may protest, 'I haven't harassed, raped or murdered anyone. The men who do are just evil.'

But masculinity needs those lone soldiers to uphold the regime. It is this background threat of violence that keeps men in power. Every time a man negotiates with a woman, like a militaristic state with its arsenal lined up behind it, he gets favourable negotiating terms because of this implicit threat.

When we are part of a culture that is ideologically extreme it is not uncommon for us to believe that, relative to our background, we are at the balanced centre. Following the Second World War, Hannah Arendt reported that, during his trial, Adolf Eichmann claimed he bore no responsibility because he was simply 'doing his job'. 'He did his duty . . . he not only obeyed orders, he also obeyed the law.'[20] She spoke of the 'banality of evil' and concluded that Eichmann was not a fanatic or sociopath, but an average person who relied on cliché defences rather than thinking for himself and was motivated by professional promotion rather than ideology.

We either need to accept there is something wrong with masculine culture or we need to accept that men are, by nature, flawed. We can't deny both.

The undeniable conclusion is that we need to confront masculinity as pathological, not just the extremes but the entire culture. Unfortunately, gender discrimination has such a powerful grip over our societal preconceptions that archaic arguments are regularly put forward for its preservation. Historical precedent is not 'nature'. If we were to argue for 'nature' in every aspect of our lives, we'd be living in caves and beating each other with clubs. In our modern world, we believe many traits can be learned, except apparently many of those that we believe are gendered. If we truly believe in meritocracy, which would lead us all to benefit from the best possible world, we need to destruct gender norms.

We hope this preface has given an objective look at the dynamics that underlie domestic abuse and its root causes. We would finally like to share a message with other victims and survivors: the bravest thing a victim can do is to speak their truth into a world that doesn't want to hear it.

Victims face a constant battle for recognition. The bravery of victims is to force us all to see the world as it is. We must all speak our truth and hold the world to account.

This is crucially important because domestic abuse is among the most underreported crimes worldwide for both men and women.[21] When men kill women and children, the victims' voices remain silent. Often, as in our case, the murderer leaves a murder note to coerce the narrative from the grave.

This book is the note that was never left by Mum and Charlotte. We hope that it can give voice to other silenced victims too.

Since our tragedy, we have been exposed to a world of passionate individuals driving for change in domestic abuse. These committed activists understand the issues at the heart of domestic abuse and how to overcome them. However, despite this wealth of knowledge, we observed a reticence in the general public to talk about domestic abuse and a reluctance to take the necessary actions required of all of us. Currently, as we look around, we see that our society is failing women and children everywhere: we have allowed women and children to become a significant refugee population within our society, fleeing male tyrants we do nothing about.

We hope that talking about our experiences can open up the conversation for others. Those who are being domestically abused reach out to family, friends and community before getting help from services. If the community does not understand domestic abuse, victims become more isolated and may never reach the services they need. In order for a conversation to happen, it is necessary that there is an informed audience to speak to and we hope our book can go some way to creating this. If there is one message that is absolutely key, it is the following: we need to talk about domestic abuse in terms of the perpetrators' demand for control, not their lack of it.

To help amplify our voices, as we seek to amplify the voices of victims everywhere, particularly those of our mother and sister, we are deeply humbled by Jeremy Corbyn's support.

Fundamentally, we hope our story can show how we had so much more in common with our mother and sister than our father.

The only things that define, divide and ally us all in this world are the choices we make and actions we take.

INTRODUCTION

'Hate destroys a man's sense of values and his objectivity.
It causes him to describe the beautiful as ugly and
the ugly as beautiful, and to confuse the true with
the false and the false with the true.'

Martin Luther King, Jr.

Our Tragedy

8:50 a.m., Tuesday 19 July 2016. The quiet market town
of Spalding was slowly waking up to a bright morning. At
the Castle Sports Complex swimming pool, some residents
were enjoying their pre-work swim while others, making
the most of the early sunshine, were pacing laps around
the nearby track in the fresh summer breeze. The pool's
car park was quiet. There were few cars and only three
people present. A blue Toyota Aygo was parked next to a
Silver Hyundai i30, boots open and their respective parking tickets purchased; one showing 8:00 a.m. and the other
8:45 a.m.

Two thunderous roars pierced through the silence,

resonating in the still air. There was a pause before a final deep shudder shook the town of Spalding. Staff from the centre and a nearby cleaner were alerted and rushed towards the sounds of gunfire. Two women were lying adjacent to each other on the floor with gunshot wounds to the abdomen. A few metres away, a deceased man was lying on the floor. The women, fifty-year-old Claire and nineteen-year-old Charlotte Hart, were regulars to the leisure centre and were instantly recognised by the staff.

Claire had suffered fatal wounds and soon passed away. Charlotte was conscious and calling for help. An air ambulance was requested and first aid administered by the attending personnel. Despite the best efforts of the courageous staff and the paramedics, as well as Charlotte's tremendous bravery and will to survive, she too passed away at the scene.

Within the hour, police had cordoned off the swimming pool and nearby schools were in lockdown. Reporters descended on Spalding. Like vultures, news helicopters circled the area in anticipation of a glimpse of the scene that had just unfolded. There was drama and excitement in the usually uneventful town of Spalding. People began speculating; theories and conspiracies were already being conceived.

Meanwhile, Luke and Ryan Hart, the two surviving sons, were working hundreds of miles away and unaware of the events that had just transpired. The news would reach them shortly. The unravelling of their traumatic past would soon begin.

*

INTRODUCTION

Claire was our mother and Charlotte our little sister.

They were our best friends and role models.

They were our inspiration and purpose in life.

The man: our father.

This is our story.

Flashback – The Burden of Birth

LUKE

'You're dead! I shot you,' Ryan insists.

'No, I dodged the bullet and now I'm on my hovercraft. You better run away fast!' I protest, charging towards Ryan.

Ryan and I are at home with our nan. She is out of her depth attempting to manage the unclear and persistently changing rules which seem to govern our aggressive playing. We're holding small action figures in our hands, but most of our playing involves us charging at each other, knocking each other to the ground and wrestling on the floor.

Playing is always, and only, competition between us. Only when one of us knows the other will win a fight do we attempt negotiation. Any peacefulness in our play is always backed up by the threat of force. Our mum bought us these toys to keep us occupied before she went to hospital.

It's now late at night and, as I'm only seven years old and Ryan five, it's much past our bedtimes. Yet, despite our intense play and the late hour, our ears are tuned for any sign of our mother's return. We've been particularly careful, even though it doesn't seem like it, not to tire ourselves out with fighting tonight because we don't want to be asleep when our mother returns.

We both hear the car pull in and the front gate open. We rush to sit down. We hear nothing for minutes, but we sit in total silence. Our eyelids are heavy, but we insist on staying awake. We are both slumped forward on the chairs, our little bodies fatigued. Ryan's eyelids are drooping now and I try to rest one eye at a time to fight sleep. Both of us are keen to look as awake as possible but are on the edge of consciousness.

The night is still as we listen closely, holding our breath each time we hear stirring outside. At last, we hear footsteps approaching the house. The door gently creaks ajar. A rush of cool, night air sweeps into the room and we are refreshed. The sweaty, stuffy air turns to a crisp, cool freshness and we hear the faint hooting of an owl in the distance among the piercing silence. We can sense the magic in the air. We are invigorated by a sudden burst of energy and sit bolt upright. Our mother's head pokes through curiously; she is surprised at the silence inside.

She smiles gently but tiredly, a glowing radiance to her face. She steps tentatively through the door carrying a small bundle in her arms. Her face is drained but satisfied. We both rush towards her and peer at our new sister, Charlotte. So delicate and beautiful, fast asleep in our mother's arms. We focus on the almost imperceptible rising and falling of Charlotte's chest as she sleeps. We are awestruck.

'She's so small!' we chime in unison.

We are amazed by Charlotte's little hands and feet and we squeeze them gently; a pulse of loving excitement rushes down our spines.

'Let me hold her!' Ryan insists.

'No, me!' I protest.

We tussle to get closer to Charlotte.

As we both stand with our mother, gaping in amazement, we feel our competitive energy fade into a deep desire to care for our new sister. This is a feeling I have not experienced before: I am used to dragging Ryan around by his feet, head banging on the floor, delivering him to our mother to resolve his crying. This was how I'd understood brotherly care; until now.

'Go to bed, it's late!'

The moment is cut short as our father comes through the front door, behind our mum. He mutters to himself and turns away from us; he shuts the door. Our expressions of awe are wiped from our faces and we quickly run up the stairs before he turns around, making each step swift but silent. We quickly get into bed and pretend to be fast asleep as we hear our father's footsteps coming closer.

That beautiful moment was so amazing but so fragile and easily shattered by our father. Our mother laboured to bring us into this world, but our father is already labouring to divide us from our little sister.

Despite our father severing our moment with Charlotte, we are curled up in bed, ecstatic. We had our fingers crossed that we would have a little sister, and what a beautiful little sister Charlotte is! But as with Ryan, Charlotte, now beautifully asleep in our mother's arms, is another mistake in our father's plans. He only needed me to make our mother dependent on him; three children are unnecessary competition with our father for our mother's affection.

1

IN THE DARK

'The line dividing good and evil cuts through the
heart of every human being.'

Aleksandr Solzhenitsyn

Our Great Escape

RYAN

Throughout June 2016, I had been commuting to Holland
for work and returning home to Spalding for the weekends. My routine was similar to when I had been working
in Reading, just a month before, so I decided to keep my
new job a secret from my father. I preferred for him to
know as little about me as possible, especially as we were
all planning to leave soon and start our new lives free from
his suffocating grasp.

I relished how Mum, Charlotte and I shared the secret
of my new job without my father knowing. We smirked
like children as I elaborately concocted stories for why I
was starting to bring my entire suitcase back with me each

weekend. Amusement was sparse when he was around. I enjoyed creating in-jokes with Mum and Charlotte or discreetly joking at my father's expense.

Planning an escape from what seemed like a maximum-security prison, adapting to a new job, company and country, while also living out of a suitcase in hotels, was exhausting. Weekends at home with Mum and my sister were closely watched by my father and allowed little chance to relax. We would be followed around the house wherever we went, sometimes blatantly and at other times shadowed from a distance. We would have to sit outside in the garden and whisper, while closely watching the back door for any signs that the predator was approaching. We learned to quickly revert to our cover conversation we had pre-agreed if he did appear; we felt like spies operating undercover in a foreign country.

I had to encrypt messages to Mum while I was away at work. The subject line and first few sentences had to be constructed so no alarms would be raised if my father stole my mum's recently obtained smartphone and saw the notification summary. We had password-protected the phone and I instructed Mum that under no circumstances was she to give the password to our father.

Hi Mum, hope you're having a great day at work. How's the weather? Work in Reading is going well. Looking forward to seeing everyone at the weekend.

Now that's out the way, here are some rental properties I've found, have a look and let's see if we can sneak in a few visits after swimming on Saturday. He shouldn't notice if we stay an extra half hour or so. If he asks, I'll just say that the club had booked our lanes for an extra 30 mins for the swim session.

LUKE

The single-carriage diesel train carried me through the flowering fields of Lincolnshire on a sunny Wednesday afternoon. The glimmer of evening light pierced through the musty windows, illuminating the coach with a deep glow. Dust danced in beautiful spirals in the air. The warm, stale air sat heavily like a blanket.

My head slumped against the jittering window and I felt immersed in drowsiness. The deep hum of the engine and caressing vibrations dissolved away my sensations. Only the flickering sun lightened my heavy eyelids. The train yielded reluctantly to the brakes. With a shudder and a deep sigh, the train pulled into the station, punctuating the end of a lazy ten-hour train journey from Scotland, where I worked.

Still intoxicated in my daze, I stirred to my feet. The doors opened and I was welcomed by the glare of the low sun. I stared through drowsy eyes and admired the beautiful sky. I saw small clouds meander in peaceful solitude across the sunset sky; the glow of radiant reds and oranges. Clusters of birds effortlessly cut through the calm in playful streaks. For once, I was no longer dissociating from the trauma of daily life. I was immersed in the tiniest details in the present moment and they all seemed so beautiful and meaningful. I no longer had to live in the future because the future we'd always planned for was about to arrive.

I was the only person there. I roused myself and wandered across the road to continue my journey to the hotel just outside of Spalding.

As I strolled through the town, I felt nostalgic as my joyful childhood memories washed over me. My mind was buoyant, and each new thought rose higher than the last. Everything was saturated with meaning. I felt like this moment was the conclusion to a long and challenging story.

I arrived at the hotel and headed up to the room. Out of the window I saw the glimmering river in the distance. The stars began to pierce through the evening sky. I collapsed into the single bed in the corner and began reading my book.

Ryan arrived. He'd flown in from Holland. There was lightness about us both. We laughed at the novelty of us both staying in a hotel room together in Spalding and made flippant jokes. Ryan came out on top as usual, as all the good ones were at my expense. We were only staying the night but somehow our things were scattered everywhere already.

We went over the plan for the next day: pick up the moving van at 8 a.m. and then head straight to the house. Our father should be at work by the time we arrived, we believed. We planned to load what we could and leave by lunch time, before he would get back.

I continued to read my book into the evening after Ryan had fallen asleep. I felt the fetters loosening and the siege of circumstance passing. Our little place in this world would become a little better after tomorrow.

On the morning of Thursday 14 July 2016, with a sense of childish eagerness, we gathered our things together and ran down for the taxi. A sense of excitement was sustaining us; we didn't need breakfast.

We signed the paperwork for the moving van, chuckled about the damage clauses (it was almost certain that I'd break something), collected the keys and went outside. It was strange to look at this vacant, yawning vehicle. Most of our lives' belongings would be in this van in the next couple of hours. It struck me how meaningless everything in it would be. All that really mattered was that Mum, Charlotte, Ryan and I would be together.

We drove to the village of Moulton and parked the van one street up from the house.

We texted Mum at the agreed time, but we didn't receive a response.

We waited a short while before we attempted to ring.
Nothing.

Ryan ran over to the house.

The car was still there and our father hadn't left. We just had to wait to see what happened next.

Fifteen minutes had passed before Mum called. Our father had driven her to work against her will in another bout of paranoia. She explained that his behaviour had been particularly bad that morning.

We collected Mum and brought her back to the house. We could only afford a couple of hours to get everything we needed into the van before he would be back for lunch. Given how agitated he was that morning, it could be less still.

Mum showed us the safe-deposit box that our father had chained up in the garage with all her personal documents and keys inside. I phoned to get a locksmith over as soon as possible to break it open. The locksmith arrived and saw the moving van outside. He saw Mum, Ryan and me sweating and rushing around. With a nod we both acknowledged what was going on and he came inside.

In the meantime, we had almost perfectly divided the belongings in two; half would remain in the house, the other half we would need to furnish the rented accommodation that Mum and Charlotte would be staying in. Mum had even left our father lunch.

We were all highly on edge. The dustbin lorry had stopped outside the house for a particularly long time. It couldn't possibly have any significance, could it? It didn't matter. I sped up.

Finally, we managed to close the sliding door on the back of the van. Mum left a note saying that she would email our father later and our dogs, Indi – a black and white Jack Russell cross – and Bella – a large, fluffy white labradoodle – hopped into the front of the van with us.

Ryan drove the van, containing everything that we now owned, to the new rental house. Charlotte at the time was on holiday with her boyfriend and would be coming back after the weekend.

Everything had been stripped bare. There we were, crammed into the front of a dusty van, nervously laughing, overcome with floods of emotion at what we had achieved. Our meagre possessions rattled behind us and our future opened widely before us. Here we were with nothing but love, yet with everything that we needed.

We'd finished unpacking by late afternoon. After takeaway pizzas, we took Indi and Bella for a walk in the park around the corner. Everything felt uncomfortably different, but I recognised that this feeling was simply freedom. An ambivalence that I had never felt or known before – the true fear and hope that come with the knowledge that we could make whatever we wished of the rest of our lives.

We were reborn.

A World Dies

RYAN

It was Tuesday 19 July in Holland. I was beaming with energy. The move had been successful and Mum and Charlotte were adapting to the start of their new lives. I had woken up at 5 a.m. to go to the gym before work. The weather was calm and there was a noticeable spring in my stride. For the first time since I could remember, I felt at peace. The future was exciting. As a family, we could finally start living.

Work was busy that morning, but around midday I found time to hurry down to the canteen and grab a quick bite to eat. Back at my desk around 11 a.m. (UK time), I needed five minutes to myself to catch my breath and zone out. Opening the BBC News app on my phone, a story caught my eye: 'Three dead in shooting in Spalding'.

The article didn't contain much information – just three or four lines of text, not revealing much more than the shooting had occurred at the Castle Sports Complex swimming pool. The article concluded by stating that more information on the breaking news story would be added when available.

I immediately messaged Mum and Charlotte. 'I heard there was a shooting at the swimming pool. Let me know that you're OK. Call me please.'

Mum was still familiarising herself with smartphones and technology. I knew it would be days before she read the message. I knew it was even more unlikely that the response I'd get would have any punctuation or capital letters and would almost certainly end with '*love mum*'. Charlotte, on the other hand, was tech-savvy like most teenage girls. A response from her would be imminent.

The panic and worry were overwhelming – I grabbed my laptop, headset, mobile phone and hurried to a nearby quiet room. The messages still both indicated *delivered* but not yet *read*. My sense of unease escalated. I decided to try to call both numbers; they rang through with no response.

Of course they wouldn't be answering, a shooting had just occurred. They would be panicked and have far more urgent concerns than answering their phones. Perhaps they were on silent or in their bags? Maybe they had both left their phones at home today?

I called Luke and explained what I'd seen. Reassuringly

he reasoned that I must be overthinking the situation and said to call the local police station who would surely refute my worries.

'Hello.'

I was met with the reassuring voice of a calm and confident young woman.

'Hi,' I said, 'I've just seen on the news that there has been a shooting in Spalding. I know my mum and sister were in the area. Can you please just confirm that they are not involved? Their names are Claire and Charlotte Hart.'

My voice was unsteady. The short pause before the woman on the end of the phone responded was excruciating.

'Can I please take your name?'

'Ryan Hart,' I choked.

'Hi, Ryan, can I take a contact number for you and I'll get someone to call you back soon?'

I gave her my mobile number and Skype work number. At this point I was beginning to get tearful. I hurried off an email to my manager to explain the situation and that I needed to take the afternoon off:

. . . even though I'm sure they're OK, I've worked myself up too much to be able to concentrate.

Scooping up my belongings from the small room, I hurried out of the office and back to the hotel, breaking into a jog once I was out of the office lobby.

Back in my hotel room I opened my laptop and placed my phone by its side, ready for the return call. I realised the chargers for both were back in the office in my bag, which I had foolishly left at my desk in the scramble to get to the quiet room. I saw that a good friend of mine, Louise, was online. I messaged her a summary of the events and explained that, although I knew they'd be fine, I might need for her to bring my bag and belongings back from the office. I didn't want to run low on battery before I received the follow-up call from the police.

I lay on my hotel bed gazing at the ceiling. My mind was racing, yet each second ticked by slower than the last. The incomprehensible chaos of thoughts made the world seem so deafening and confusing.

I was roused by the ringing of my phone. My focus narrowed and suddenly my mind cleared. The anticipation of this phone call now turned to fear. The entire world suddenly consisted of myself, now sitting upright on the bed, and the phone, summoning for me to answer.

'Hello,' I anxiously answered.

'Hello, is this Ryan Hart?' It was a woman, but somebody different, not the one I had spoken to earlier.

'Yes.'

'Where are you and do you have anyone with you?'

'I'm in Holland and, no, I'm by myself.' My answer surprised her – she obviously expected me to be in Lincolnshire.

'Holland?! Ah, OK. Do you have any siblings or other immediate family members and contact details for them too?'

The woman was calm and reassuring. She was professional and led me through the series of questions. The request for contact information for Luke, Charlotte's boyfriend and other members of my immediate family should have confirmed my worst suspicions but instead my mind decided to ignore what was happening. There was a huge elephant in the small hotel room and its presence was squeezing the life out of me. She agreed to call me back soon and I retreated to my bed. The conversation had been both confusing and vague. I still knew nothing about what had happened and why I couldn't get hold of my mum and sister. My mind continued to cling to delusion, convincing me that, come Friday, I'd be back with my mum and Charlotte for our first weekend in our new home together.

The phone rang again. This time the voice on the end of the phone was familiar. It was a man, in fact a colleague of my mum's and one of her best friends. He explained that he was at Spalding police station. This was followed by a lengthy pause. I could hear his breathing was accelerated.

The next five words would shatter my delusions and force me to accept the unbearable truth. He sounded strong and supportive, yet I could tell that he too was afraid. With a trembling voice, he spoke.

'Come home, mate. Come home.'

My mother and little sister had been murdered.

LUKE

I missed the first call on my mobile. It was a number that I didn't recognise, and I rarely answered my phone anyway.

Before I could put my mobile down, my work phone began to ring.

I immediately heard Ryan's choked voice on the other end: 'Have you seen the news?'

'No, not yet . . .'

I loaded the news app on my mobile. The top story: 'Shooting in Spalding'.

The moment hung precipitously. I felt off-balance.

My heart flushed a wave of piercing cold throughout my entire body. I noticed that my hands had begun to shake vigorously.

'Oh yeah, I see.'

The words that came from my mouth were calm, but my trembling voice wasn't reassuring. I was observing my mind and my body operating separately, yet I felt that neither were truly me. I searched for a simple explanation that this wasn't what I thought. I had to interpret this differently. It couldn't be Mum and Charlotte. For a second, my mind forced me to think it was them. But that couldn't be the case? Someone somewhere had to have made a mistake. This was a joke. Intricate and elaborate, but a joke nonetheless.

'Oh no. It's erm . . .' I said dismissively. I discounted the entire moment. I discounted what felt like reality but wasn't.

I realised that I hadn't taken a breath as my body gasped for air. In that moment, my perception of reality suddenly snapped. I felt like everything was happening somewhere else. I was stuck somewhere beyond reality.

Ryan's voice crashed through my distraction: 'I can't get hold of Mum or Charlotte.'

'Oh. Let's. Let's erm . . .' I paused. 'Just check with the police. It won't be what you think but it's worth just ringing up and checking that it's not them.'

'OK. OK.' I heard a slight relief but still a profound sadness in Ryan's voice.

I looked up the Spalding police number and called. I got up and rushed to the corridor for some privacy. I felt like I was using absolutely no energy. I felt ethereal; like no one was noticing me.

'Hello.'

'Hi. I just saw there was a shooting in Spalding and want to check that my mum and sister are OK. They were around that area. That's all.'

There! There was a tiny hesitation. My heart skipped but then the lady started to talk.

'OK, can I take your name please?'

'Luke Hart.'

There it was. The same pause again.

'Erm, OK, who would you like to check about?' The voice on the other end sounded unprepared for what might come next.

I paused.

'Erm, Charlotte.'

'Is that your sister?'

Now I felt my heart smashing against my ribs. It was getting faster and faster, ready to pop. How did she know that? Was it a guess? Why were they guessing?

I couldn't hear anything except my heart beating. I raised my voice over the pounding blood in my ears.

'Yes, and my mum, Claire.'

I gave the lady my phone number and she said that she would contact me shortly.

I noticed that I was walking much faster than I had started. I carried on walking for another five minutes.

I felt like I was grabbing at the time ahead of me and tearing it into the past. I just needed them to ring me and say that everything was fine. I was becoming aggravated.

It was blinding sun outside; it was the middle of the day. Yet, I felt like it was 10 p.m. I could have slept for a week. The sun was oppressive. Its sharp brightness pierced into my sickened stomach and made me want to vomit. Even squinting left me feeling exhausted.

I got a lift back to the flat, overcome with disbelief and adrenaline. When I arrived I rushed inside and collapsed on the sofa. I placed my phone on the table in front of me. I hunched forward and stared at it, slumped from the fatigue caused by keeping my body operating at this level. I just needed to lie down. I needed to let whatever was happening resolve itself. I was so painfully confused. I felt a rising sickness and an acid burning through my organs. The adrenaline was now failing to protect me.

The phone rang.

'Is that Luke?'

'Yes.'

'Do you have anyone with you?'

In that moment, my mind and my body collided. I couldn't speak. Suddenly I knew my brain had to process what it had been avoiding.

I was entirely within myself, in a world where I had no words to describe what I saw. I was a newborn child gazing with confusion into a bleak world that I could not comprehend. A panic rose strongly within, a desire to mould the world back to how it should have been. But this world was no longer mine.

Everything froze.

Like a small, lonely child, I stood in silence in the infinite darkness.

A Journey to Nowhere

RYAN

'Louise?' I typed.

'Yes, Ryan. Everything OK?'

I paused, unsure of what to say. I couldn't even comprehend the situation myself and so had no idea how to convey it.

With difficulty, I typed:

'It's them.'

'I'm on my way. Stay where you are. I'll be with you soon.'

My breathing was laboured, I had to shower and change out of my work clothes: I felt suffocated by them. I needed to find some normality in the situation, even if it was just the clothes I was wearing.

I changed into shorts, a t-shirt and flip-flops. I called up the travel agent to change my return flight to London City airport to the next available one that day, departing 6:15 p.m., UK time, from Rotterdam airport.

There was a knock on the door. I answered to see Louise

standing there, clutching my bag. I had only met Louise four weeks ago when I started my new job in Holland. She introduced me to the team and made me feel at home. Now, with my home as I previously knew it shattered, and suddenly with an immense responsibility thrust upon her, Louise stood before me with a look of compassion and fortitude in her eyes. She immediately launched herself at me, giving me a reassuring, lengthy hug. No words were said; no words needed to be said.

Louise agreed to come with me for support. There were a few hours before we needed to leave to catch the flight, much of which was spent lying on the bed staring at the hotel ceiling. Whenever I tried to move, dizziness overcame me and I felt like I would faint.

Louise had hurried back to her room to grab her passport, arranged a taxi and helped pack my bags. I was guided down to reception to check out and we made our way to the airport.

Delayed due to a technical fault.

Checked in and having made our way through security to the most secluded part of the airport we could find, this was not the message I needed to see.

Over the last month, my flights had regularly been delayed from twenty minutes to a couple of hours due to issues that summer at London City airport. We were booked on the last flight from Rotterdam. I needed to catch this flight.

The airport staff calmly repeated a carefully rehearsed

statement whenever we enquired about the length of the delay and the exact issue. Louise was scanning flights from other airports in the country and preparing a plan B in case the *technical* issue was irreparable. There was a flight from Amsterdam to London Stansted, due to depart in a few hours, and this was the last remaining flight back to England that evening. We both knew that, should our flight be officially cancelled, there were close to one hundred people in the waiting lounge anticipating and preparing for the same outcome. In fact, some were already heading over to Amsterdam. Unfortunately, I had checked in bags and was unable to get them back until a formal decision had been made on the status of our flight.

All the while, Louise had been coordinating with both a family liaison officer and my previous manager from my job in Reading. They were due to meet us at London City airport and were kept in the loop about the delays. Luke had flown from Aberdeen and was waiting at London City airport with them.

The inevitable confirmation came. The flight was cancelled. Pandemonium ensued as everyone hurried back out to the front desk to queue up and hear what options they had. We were in the queue, but we could hear that the fellow passengers in front were being offered dinner, a hotel room and the first flight back to London in the morning.

Thankfully I had Louise with me. I was broken. I had no idea what to do. I wanted to collapse on the floor and cry.

'The flight from Amsterdam boards in just over an hour. Let's grab your bags as soon as they come out and call up a taxi to be here waiting for us.'

We knew that our chances of getting a taxi from the rank outside, once the entire population from the cancelled flight decided to either rush to Amsterdam or reluctantly head to their arranged hotel room, would be slim. We arranged for a car to meet us outside the airport entrance and hoped that the checked-in bags would soon be available for us to collect.

A member of staff proceeded to bring out trolleys piled high with the checked-in bags as I received a phone call; the taxi had just arrived outside. Before I could even catch my breath, Louise had grabbed my bags and we hurried outside and into the taxi.

I gazed out through the car's window, as it raced across the country, feeling like there was nowhere in the world I belonged. Nowhere left for me to call home. Nowhere for me to hurry to.

Louise was busy on the phone, working magic behind the scenes to arrange for our flight and arrival in London. As we were so close to the boarding time for the flight, it wasn't possible to book over the phone. However, Louise was prepared with the exact location of where we needed to go in the airport once we arrived.

As the taxi screeched to a stop, I jumped out and headed to the boot while Louise paid for the journey.

'There's only ten minutes 'til boarding. We can book you on the flight, but you have to be really quick to get to the gate on time,' the lady at the check-in desk explained.

Finally, some good news. Bags checked in, we hurried to security to find a sizeable queue. Without hesitation, Louise rushed us to the front and threw our belongings onto the conveyor belt. Nobody asked questions – they could tell there was good reason for our impoliteness. Either from my bloodshot eyes or the look of unrelenting determination on Louise's face, it was evident we didn't have the time or energy to explain ourselves.

Fumbling around for my belongings on the other side of the scanner, it was clear that I was in no fit state as I attempted and failed to thread my belt back through the loops on my shorts. Louise noticed my distress, grabbed everything else and left me with just a simple job: follow her while putting my belt on. Surely, I could manage that?

No. No I couldn't.

For someone with such a petite build, Louise had speed! It also didn't help that my choice of footwear didn't lend itself to athletics; my shorts were slightly oversized, and I'd only managed to get the belt threaded halfway round. Clutching my flip-flops in one hand and holding my half-done-up shorts with the other, I ran the best I could. In hindsight, flip-flops were a terrible choice. Although, it must have been an amusing sight for any bystanders.

The gate was the other side of Amsterdam airport and the airport was much larger than I had anticipated. Sweating profusely, we made it, just. We boarded the aircraft, and both took a deep sigh of relief. We were on our way to London.

In the row behind us there was an autistic child, sitting with her parents. She was interested in me and decided she wanted to teach me my name in sign language. I learned how to sign her name too. Engaging with this girl reminded me of the kindness and compassion that my mother and sister radiated every day. Charlotte had always found joy in helping those less fortunate than herself and had regularly volunteered at a local special needs school. Our mother had learned to sign to communicate with a deaf customer she'd regularly see at work once a week. Both would, without hesitation, go out of their way to bring even just the slightest ray of sunshine into someone else's day.

Having touched down at London Stansted airport and been instructed by the beep of the seatbelt sign, everyone mustered to their feet. Out of the window I could see two smartly dressed women with a police officer standing at the base of the stairs. A voice came over the PA system.

'Please can everyone take their seats for just a moment.'

A curious silence swept through the fuselage and within moments everyone was back in their seats.

'Are Ryan and Louise onboard?'

I raised my hand. We grabbed our bags and headed to the front of the plane. I could feel the eyes of the fellow passengers follow us. At the base of the stairs we were met by two family liaison officers, one of whom was the woman I had been speaking to on the phone when I was back in my hotel room in Holland. I apologised for the flight being late (a typical British response given everything that had happened that day) and reached out my hand to greet Di and Debs.

'Come here,' Di gasped, pushing my hand to the side and jumping in for a heartfelt embrace.

We were led through the airport by the police officer, bypassing any barriers and queues. We handed our boarding passes to the officer and were assured that our bags would be delivered to the police station where we were headed.

Luke was outside waiting beside two unmarked police cars. The last time we had seen each other was just two days before. We had been sitting in the living room of our small rented house, boxes piled high against the walls waiting to be unpacked, our dogs running around and licking our faces. Those days and evenings had been filled with laughter. We could sense for the first time in our mum's adult life that her joy was completely absent of fear and worry. The memory of us all parting ways on that Sunday was still fresh in my mind. I hadn't anticipated seeing Luke again so soon. I hadn't expected that parting to be the last time I would ever see my mother.

LUKE

I was aware that anything that I was able to do was meaningless. With a jolt, my entire past revolved into an entirely new perspective: I saw pure evil in clear sight that had previously lived hidden from my view. I realised that my family had been host to a parasite.

I couldn't imagine what had happened. My mind was either protecting me or it simply couldn't comprehend.

Eventually I stopped crying.

I ordered a taxi, grabbed a small backpack and threw in a handful of books and a phone charger. Everything I had seemed worthless, but books always helped me understand the world. Maybe they'd have the answers I needed now.

The taxi came, and I asked to go to the airport in the fewest words possible. It was one of the warmest days of the year. The taxi driver was chirpy and began a conversation. I tried to engage but words made me feel sick. A tear ran down my face. I didn't feel that I was crying but my eyes were red-raw.

The taxi driver saw and apologised. I explained simply that I had received sad news. He understood and asked if they were important to me. I nodded. The rest of the journey continued in silence as I let the pain ease out, one lonely tear at a time.

I arrived in the airport and asked for the next flight to London. I headed over to the café, grabbed a coffee and sat in the far corner. I gently sobbed to vent the explosive cocktail of rage, grief and helplessness.

Over the radio I heard the morning's events. I held my hands against my ears even though I could have guessed exactly what they were saying.

Time blurred past.

The next thing I remember, I was landing at London City airport. Before anyone had an opportunity to stand up, there was an announcement that we needed to wait for a while. I saw the stewardess make eye contact and walk purposefully towards me. As she approached she tentatively whispered, 'Luke?'

I nodded, and she turned and indicated that I follow. Two female police officers and two male police officers stood at the exit to the plane.

I was escorted into a conference room in the airport. As soon as I was seated, I gave a rapid summary of our life and our father to the police officers. They must have expected pleasantries, even in a situation like this: they scrambled for pens and rushed to take notes.

We heard that Ryan had managed to get the last flight from Holland to Stansted. There was a coordinated rush around me. Yet I felt as if I was trapped inside the silent, motionless eye of the storm. I was placed in a car and the world continued to move under my feet as I remained dazed, frozen.

We arrived at Stansted. It was now getting dark. I saw Ryan stumbling towards us in broken flip-flops and baggy shorts with his huge suitcase. We hugged. There were no words we could say to acknowledge this moment.

We were taken to a local police station that evening where it was explained what would happen to us over the coming days and weeks.

Nothing stuck in my turbulent mind. It was too busy throwing things off to be able to take anything in.

Reunion

Our dogs, Bella and Indi, had been collected from the rental house and were in police kennels.

The first few days following the murders were spent giving statements recalling our lives. We were also required to identify Charlotte's body at the morgue. This was the first time our tragedy became truly real to us. Seeing Charlotte shook us to the core. How could someone do something so horrific to someone so beautiful? We had been advised not to see the body of our mother due to her injuries, and the horror of it all made us shudder.

At each encounter with the police we asked if we could see the dogs. Eventually, after persistent nagging, particularly from Ryan, we were granted our request.

We pulled into the police car park to collect Indi and Bella. They looked dejected and lost, both sitting behind the cage bars with a distant, passive look in their eyes. A bittersweet love washed over us. We could sense the same invisible support between them both that we had for each other.

We were informed that the car the police had ferried us in was rented and that we needed to be careful not to get dog hair in it. We agreed, even though both sides knew the agreement was predominantly phatic.

Indi and Bella still hadn't noticed us as we moved towards the cage. The cage was opened and they tentatively wandered out.

The instant they spotted us they both erupted with energy. Indi darted from person to person, licking ankles and panting heavily. Bella, however, ignored everyone and bolted straight for the car, leaping in through the open front passenger's door. In a frenzy of fluff, she dived between the seats as we all tried to catch her.

As Ryan and I stepped back with childish giggles, there was a flash of panic on Di's and Deb's faces before the futility of it all became clear.

We all stood and smiled. Bella planted her head on the open window. With wide eyes and flapping tongue, she gazed towards us in satisfied exhaustion.

'If only Mum and Charlotte could be here to see this with us too,' we thought.

An Unreal Reality

RYAN

'White lilies for Mum, orange chrysanthemums for Charlotte.'

Kate, a good family friend, was handing out the *boutonnières* to the eight pallbearers: Luke, myself, Ben (Charlotte's boyfriend) and five of our childhood friends.

Emotions overwhelmed me and I had to run upstairs; reality had hit. My mother and sister were gone, they were now merely represented by flowers. For the past four weeks, my mind had refused to accept the truth, that the future I had spent twenty-five years fighting for was no more. The only mechanism my mind could muster was to switch off; switch off and pretend that I was existing temporarily in some other world, a dream perhaps, from which I would soon wake up.

The two hearses arrived. Inside each, a beautiful wicker casket. I couldn't bring myself to walk outside and stand by the hearses. Inside were the bodies of the two most important women in my life. The two women whom I had felt responsible for. I had failed them. The last time I had seen Charlotte's face was at the morgue. She was lying there, so peacefully, so beautifully – as if she was just sleeping: I wanted to wake her.

The police had closed off the main road through the village, from Kate's house all the way to the church. Residents of Moulton were standing on the edge of their drives, heads bowed, as the procession made its way towards the church.

'Canon in D' rang out from the church organ as, step by step, we shouldered the wicker caskets past the filled pews towards the stands at the front of the church.

With Mum and Charlotte resting side by side, I took my seat.

Nothing could prepare me for the anguish and the unbearable amalgamation of emotions I was to experience during the ceremony; I felt the most vulnerable I had ever been in my life.

LUKE

Each step I took broke through the sense of disbelief, but it quickly returned. I felt that I could float around like a wisp in the wind. I was no longer a part of my body and was separate from what had been the concerns of my life. The only thing that made me feel real was the vacillating yet burning anger, yet even that felt ethereal too.

How did our lives lead to this?

I kept my eyes firmly planted on the hearse in front. There was no 'why?' There was simply the disbelief in the power of questioning at all. Everything which I once believed made me strong, which affected the world and made me safe, was gone. I was unable to protect the people whom I cared most about in the world. In a single moment on 19 July, the brittle link between cause and effect was broken. The world seemed to be unfolding regardless of my intentions, like I was simply a spectator to the events of my life.

I looked over and saw Ryan overwhelmed with sadness. I continued to flicker between anger and nothing at all. I was angry at this lie, this life. I realised that while I was experiencing abstraction, alienation and disconnectedness, Ryan was still firmly planted in the world, with the courage to bear what had happened to us. Ryan was always the strongest of us. I gave punches, but Ryan could take them. I chose my battles only when I was certain I could win. Ryan always took life on its own terms.

As we took the caskets into the church, the flashes of media cameras did nothing to punctuate the vagueness that overwhelmed me. The delirium glazed over all I could possibly feel. My mind refused to pay attention to any details at all. It intended to remember as little of this as possible.

On our shoulders were the women whom we had spent our lives protecting. My body had relinquished its duty to convey any information to me about my brutal existence. All I knew was that moment felt both real and unreal. Both states existed strangely comfortably side by side. Contradictions seemed to make more sense than reason.

As the service began, once again I felt myself crash back down to earth from my detached vantage point. Through the tenseness of my body I felt my emotions bubble up as my emotional barrier fatigued. Suddenly, an overwhelming torrent washed over me as I could no longer hold it back. I involuntarily slumped in on myself as my body gave up its final strength.

I noticed a feeling that, at first, I didn't understand but then it became lucidly clear. I was a boy again. I was that same vulnerable young boy who has been pretending he was strong for so long. I was that same boy who I saw in those moments where life demonstrated that it is I who obeyed its rules and not the other way around.

All I wanted were the two women whom we had carried here, who were now at the front of the church. I broke down and cried.

My chest heaved as my body purged the poison of my past. At last, I was in my body, but my control had been entirely relinquished. I couldn't possibly know how to deal with this – I just had to let it all happen. As if I had any alternative.

As our bodies were awash with anguish, our eulogy was read out against the backdrop of solemn silence, broken by the rising and falling of our heaving sobs:

What can be said about Mum and Charlotte is bounded by the limits of language and the reaches of our own expression. Charlotte and Mum are more beautiful than the words that can be drawn upon to paint their images. Connecting with other people can sometimes be the most difficult part of life. It can sometimes feel that the capacity to express how much you care is not there; that there aren't enough words, enough colours, enough closeness, no matter how hard you squeeze. Mum and Charlotte lived through acts of compassion. They lived virtuously through instinct; it was so beautifully natural to them both.

Mum would always be so proud of her children and we would all be so proud of her. Everything good in us is her, everything that we have ever achieved is because of her inspiration. Her children are all creations of her love and through us you may see into the power of her heart. Never have we met anyone who is so defined by their capacity to love, whose entire essence is love.

When Charlotte joined us, we couldn't believe something so beautiful, kind and delicate could exist in the world. Ever since she was a small child, Charlotte dedicated herself to looking after the vulnerable and had an affinity and such a unique connection with animals. Charlotte had a wicked sense of humour. We were always surprised and amused that such a sweet face could deliver such powerful sarcasm. Charlotte inspired us to be the best we could be, to be role models for her. We grew into men for her.

As was evident to all who knew them, Mum and Charlotte lived and loved unconditionally. When you care about someone so deeply, as we did for them, such unconditionality can sometimes be painful to endure. You wish the best for those you love and they are busy giving it to everyone, often at their own expense. But they were always at their happiest when they made others happy. Their kind eyes gave them away. They sowed the seeds of compassion in the world around them and never tore the beautiful flowering plants from the earth for themselves. We can only hope that, when our time comes, we have been able to understand life as they did and to give as readily and generously as they did.

Summer's fragrant flowers are too beautiful and too delicate to survive the cruel winter storms. It takes indescribable braveness to choose the vulnerability to be that beautiful in a world that can be so cruel. Mum and Charlotte chose to be that beautiful. They transcended life. They learned to create the sun in the winter gloom. They blossomed through every day and night and through every season. They created a world that revolved around them. We chose them over the world.

It feels so unreal to talk about them like they're not here. It feels like they haven't gone. When we listen, when we look deeply, we realise that they haven't. They never left; they created us with parts of themselves. We feel them in our actions, in our hopes and in our compassion.

Life is at its most difficult when you are confronted with its impermanence. Life is the things we can't keep; it is the things that we must give away. It is the water that slips between our fingers or the evening sunlight that passes into darkness. For our most treasured possessions to grow they must be let outside into the sunlight, to be shown to the world. They can't survive in the darkness of our grasp, in the staleness of our possession. Mum and Charlotte have left their imprint on the world, not by stamping their feet into the soil, but by becoming the winds that shape it. Through their lives and the influence that they had over us, they have become the eternal forces that shape us, that shape our world.

Thank you for everything that you showed us and

taught us. You showed that a life isn't measured by how much you can take, but by how much you can give. You gave us everything even when nothing was guaranteed in return, and for that you have been welcomed deep within us. More than we were ever amazed by the mysteries of the universe or the gift of life, we were always awestruck that the universe could create something as beautiful as you both.

We know that right now you will both be looking upon us and wishing us the strength to carry on. We owe you everything we have to keep going, to not be defeated. With your love, inspiration and determination as an example we have been shown a resilience that cannot be matched. We hope to make you as proud as you have made us. We love you, Mum. We love you, Charlotte.

The tears continued until our tear ducts ached. All that could pierce the fatigue was faint shivering. Yet, among the utter exhaustion there was at last a faint sense of peace. The tenseness of striving to be outside of ourselves had passed.

We felt grateful for everything our mother and Charlotte had given us. We felt the relinquishing of memories of our father.

We were beginning to see things slightly differently. In our minds there was a faint looseness of perspective. We felt the lies unravelling, some our own delusions, and some our father's, as our minds at last dared to attempt to make sense of this.

That evening we sat at the wake, hosted at the local sports park where, as children, we spent many of our evenings playing. After many had left and only a few re-mained, we saw the setting sun radiate through the leaves of the great oak trees. But we didn't see the light. We felt it. We noticed how it reached deep beyond our sore eyes. We experienced the light and somehow it warmed our souls. We were comforted, and we felt the essence of our mother and sister inside of us. As we said in our eulogy, they created us with parts of themselves.

In that moment, we felt the faint beginnings of hope. In what seemed like utter darkness, we began to see the guiding light of our mother and sister to save us. We both needed each other. Indi and Bella needed us, and we needed them. We had reasons to be here.

We committed to do everything that we could to over-come all that had led to this. We committed to learn how to live and lead each other from here. We would make the best of this world.

The one thing we refused to do was to give up.

Flashback – Fathering Fear

RYAN

'Cool, a horror movie about spiders! I want to watch it!' I boast with confidence, flicking through the TV magazine at lunch time, barely five years old. I puff my shoulders back and with a nonchalant smile I look up, expecting everyone to welcome in my coming of age.

'Ryan, you're far too young and it's on way past your

bedtime,' my mother protests, aware of what is to come next.

She is immediately shouted down by our father for interfering. Our father's face lights up with a sly smile and he leans back slowly in his chair. 'It'll be good for the boy.'

Our mother's eyes drop to the table and she quietly continues eating her lunch. Our father pauses a while longer and fixes a satisfied stare on me.

It's rare my father lets me do things against the rules, particularly staying up later. I'm surprised but excited. I'm eager to grow up, I'm keen to prove I'm strong.

That afternoon, I don't notice my father. He gives me an unusual freedom and I feel my confidence building throughout the day. Now I'm ready to show everyone I can handle it: a real horror movie.

It's nine o'clock and it looks like everyone else has gone to bed. I sit down and turn on the TV. As the film starts, I'm amazed that I'm able to watch this. I'm not even scared, I'm a grown-up at last!

Suddenly, a giant spider eats one of the characters and I burst into tears. I'm running out of the room when my father steps into the doorway and gestures back towards the seat.

'Come on, Ryan, it's just starting. You're not leaving now, are you?'

I'm still crying and want to leave but I see he won't move. I still hear the screaming and shrieking coming from the TV. My mind is rushing with terrifying images, but I slowly shake my head and turn to sit down again.

This time, he follows and sits in the corner, watching me. I feel so confused. I felt so brave before, but now I feel so scared. I realise I can't leave, so try to pretend I'm not scared. If I wince, he scowls. I watch the film, no longer crying, but with the fear deep inside.

I'm acutely aware of the darkness and the silence around me, punctuated by the sudden bright lights and screeching noises from the film. My mind is racing faster and faster as it becomes hyperaware of my surroundings, looking for danger everywhere.

The film ends.

'Not so bad, was it?' my father smirks contentedly at his achievement. I see on his face that he knows this fear he is brewing is something he can use later; he knows it is useful to teach fear young, while I'm still malleable. He turns off the TV and the lights and wanders up to bed.

I remain on the couch, frozen in a disconcerting silence and darkness. My mind is still racing with terrifying images. The world seems scarier now. Everything I don't know or don't see feels dangerous. I scold myself for thinking I was brave; I won't ever do that again.

With a five-year-old's thousand-yard stare, I gaze emptily at the TV as I feel the arachnophobia scuttling around my insides. My eyes are now dry but my insides are aflame. I see my faint reflection in the TV from the pale moonlight coming through the window. My face looks harder now but my insides feel torn to shreds. I look like a man but I'm not a man.

I never will be.

Operation Lighthouse

We spent the following weeks recounting our lives to the police to form our statements. As we spoke, we began to unravel hidden motives and lies embedded within a false world that had been constructed by our father.

We would often be forced to admit that moments that we considered to be pleasant from our youth were in fact tainted with our father's malevolent intentions. We were simply controlled like puppets to achieve his ends under contrived narratives. We slowly learned that we were victims of domestic abuse, something we had never considered before.

During these days, we often heard and saw the words, 'Operation Lighthouse'. These were the words stamped onto a burgeoning file of police documents. Words randomly chosen to name our family's tragedy; the meaningless title to a meaningless act. Words of light and clarity to describe something so dark and messy. A metaphor for staunch resilience to darkness to describe us at our most vulnerable.

These words, 'Operation Lighthouse', felt so intimidating juxtaposed with our weakness. They seemed to be another element of reality that made no sense. What did it mean to be alive but not understand the context of our lives? Were we alive at all? Had we ever been?

Growing up, we had never identified as victims of domestic abuse and did not realise the mortal danger that our family was in. We had not heard anyone speak about domestic abuse and didn't have the constructs to understand what we were living through. We believed that domestic abuse involved drunken fathers beating their families every weekend, something that would be clear to everyone, particularly those suffering its consequences. We had always interpreted our father's behaviour as unpleasant, disrespectful and aggressive, but never dangerous. We were constantly fed the narrative by our father that these were the 'normal ups and downs of family life' and that we had no alternative, which unfortunately we didn't.

Yet, we survived and struggled powerfully onwards because of the inspiration we derived from of our mother and sister; they were our archetypes of virtue throughout it all. Through the meaning they found in their actions and from the abundance they gave to the world, they showed us that there was another, better way to live even despite the evil and misfortune we had suffered. Mum and Charlotte always remained positive despite our father's corrosive behaviours, pouring love into our dogs and, despite our father's financial control, selling what little they had at car boot sales and donating the money to charity. They always found a way to shine light into darkness and they kept us both steady through the turbulent storms our father created every day. They drew the focus of our attention as we learned to ignore our father.

The lethal outcomes of domestic abuse often leave our society shocked, particularly with coercive control. We had never even heard of coercive control, yet this was a phrase that characterised our entire existence. We thought domestic abuse was about physical confrontations and fights. We had never realised that it could also be about systematically controlling the lives of family members so that they gradually lose their autonomy and sense of who they are. We had never perceived that a father would wish to strip his family of financial resources on purpose, to destroy their self-esteem, to sever their support networks and systematically eliminate their human rights. We couldn't believe that a father would attempt to reduce the life of his family to one of mere slaves. We never considered it, so we never saw it, even though it was right in front of us.

However, we came to realise that what appears to be a lack of visible abuse may be indicative of the very abuse suffered. A family that is always together may be one that is not permitted to be apart. A family which always seems to follow the rules could be one terrified of the consequences should they be broken. A family that struggles to leave an abusive father may have no resources to do so.

It became clear from our previous misunderstandings and from the reactions of the media that domestic abuse is an iceberg, the largest piece of it shrouded below the waterline of ignorance. After our own ignorance was shattered, we couldn't even begin to comprehend the scale of suffering that must exist from a cause that is hidden from both victims and society. How much suffering exists below this waterline when we do not even see that which is above? How many lives are submerged into the non-fatal but life-changing trauma caused by such invisible abuse?

Our tragedy unveiled to us the lethal dangers posed by coercive control. It laid bare the true perils posed by an unyielding, patriarchal masculinity which demands total control or death. Only in research after our tragedy did we come to learn that coercive control is a more accurate predictor of domestic homicide than is sustained domestic violence, because it reveals the perpetrator's belief that they are entitled to control the life of their victim, not simply to hurt them.[1]

Our investigations have revealed to us how coldly conceived belief systems are more dangerous than searing emotion, despite emotion often being held accountable for male violence instead of the men themselves. Murder of women by men is often defended and excused as if it was caused by 'snapping', 'flipping out' or a 'loss of control'. The intent of these defences of violent male behaviour, readily repeated by the public and media, is to demonstrate that men are often provoked by victims beyond any ability to exercise their will and agency. Despite these excuses referring to the emotional equivalent of man flu – that men, unlike women, 'understandably' just flip out violently sometimes, something women could obviously never understand – the 'loss of control' defence reveals more than it possibly intends. We learned that the true reason men kill women and children in domestic homicide has nothing to do with torrents of emotion. It is due to a purposeful agency which demands death where male control over patriarchal subordinates has been lost. These men believe they have the right to control women and children. They refuse to sacrifice their privilege and will readily kill in cold blood, including themselves if required, to reinforce male familial dominance and intimidate others from challenging it.

We had believed that we weren't in physical danger

because we thought an escalation of violence in our home would have to happen first. We had believed that for someone to murder they had to have the taste of blood to initiate their frenzy. We thought our father would have to 'lose control' of his mind to hurt us. These myths blinded us to the true danger posed by coercive control. Whether these murderous men are aware of the belief systems driving their actions is another question, but it is clear to us now that belief systems, not emotions, are responsible for domestic homicides.

As men having suffered under this broken masculine ideology, we realised that we needed to help change the wider conversation. Domestic abuse truly is terrorism. NATO defines terrorism in the AAP-06 NATO Glossary of Terms and Definitions, Edition 2014, thus: 'The unlawful use or threatened use of force or violence against individuals or property in an attempt to coerce or intimidate governments or societies to achieve political, religious or ideological objectives.' We would argue that the control and violence exercised by men against women and children in domestic abuse is consistent with achieving a political and ideological end through mass terror. Its goal is to deprecate the position of women in society through fear and control. Once fear has been established, it is no longer necessary to exert violence because the fear of violence becomes internalised in the victim and they begin to constrain themselves, its effect always present if not visible.

It could be argued that religiously motivated terrorism is but a subset of the consistent thread which runs through all terrorism – gender violence. Often after a terrorist event is committed, the perpetrator's history of domestic abuse is unearthed. In fact, studies of mass shootings in the United States from 2009 to 2016 have shown that 54 per cent of cases of terrorism were related to domestic or family violence.[2] The total yearly economic cost to the UK (through impact on GDP growth, on the criminal justice system; physical costs of homicides, injuries and property damage, and wider psychological effects) from domestic abuse is over twenty times that of conventional terrorism (£66bn[3] compared to £3.2bn[4]).

The UK government's annual spending on each issue is in the region of £0.04bn for domestic abuse and £2bn for conventional terrorism.[5] This is not to say that conventional terrorism isn't an issue. On the contrary, we recognise that conventional terrorism inflicts huge suffering and damage on individuals and society. However, when we strip all acts of evil bare and examine the fundamental principles of humanity, which are to minimise suffering and injustice, we realise that our society's attention is heavily prejudiced and not focused objectively. In 2017 alone, a total of 105 women were killed by male partners or ex-partners in the UK.[6] This is greater than all deaths from terrorism from 2006 to 2018 in the UK.[7]

Domestic abuse is not rooted in intractable, evolutionary, emotional problems within men, but in belief systems and therefore we have a responsibility to change these beliefs to save lives. Martin Luther King, Jr. said, 'Injustice anywhere is a threat to justice everywhere.'[8] If we choose not to challenge abuse, the rot of injustice and inequality will spread.

Therefore, we must begin to hold men accountable for their actions. In attempting to rationalise domestic homicide by drawing causal links between events, we miss the underlying truth that actions are not caused by events, but that events are caused by the decisions and actions of individuals. Circumstances are in many ways incidental. Many men choose not to kill when they become divorced. They choose not to kill when they are having financial difficulties. We all choose to become who we are. Killers have chosen to become killers. They were not coerced by circumstances. In fact, it is likely that they created the circumstances which they use as their excuses.

Our father's behaviour was the result of an active choice that he made every day. He chose to lay the burden of his existence upon us. But where he attempted to crush us, we learned to lift the unbearable weights and became stronger than he could have ever imagined. We hope that our lives can inspire others to overcome their challenges and retain hope in a better world, if they are willing to act in service of it.

Flashback – Hammer Home

RYAN

I want to play on the old PlayStation but Charlotte has reactively decided she wants to watch the TV instead.

I'm eleven, and Charlotte is six. To be honest, I don't mind what we do as long as something distracts me from the crashing noises of Dad hammering away upstairs at the walls.

The house we have just moved into in Moulton needs a lot of work doing, most of which Mum, Luke, Charlotte and I are dragged into helping with. All morning Luke and I had to rake an enormous gravel pile across the front of the house and help move bricks around to put up a wall across the driveway. We frequently crossed the line from 'inside father', yelling and criticising as we gathered the materials from the back garden, to 'outside father', smiling and jovially chatting to passers-by as, brick by brick, he built the façade the world was allowed to see and marvel at.

Now is my break and I want to relax.

What is annoying me, however, is that Charlotte seems not to care what is on the TV; she just wants to stop me playing my game and to annoy me.

Charlotte and I often enjoy winding each other up. It's working. Neither of us is that interested in the outcome, we've found enjoyment in annoying each other. It has become a game in itself. With no intention of resolving the argument, we both begin laughing and pretending we are the victim. Really, we just want to have a laugh with Mum too.

'Mum! *Muuuummmmmm! Muuuuuumm!*' we both holler in between laughter.

Mum arrives and sees Charlotte and me trying to pull angry faces at each other, but smirks break through.

Mum comes in with a smile on her face because she's seen this too many times and knows what we're up to. We are all laughing at our attempts to amuse ourselves in the barren, construction zone of a house we are residing in. Suddenly, crashing through the joy, a bellowing call chills me to the bone.

'BOY! Get upstairs now!'

I hang my head and shuffle out of the living room and look upstairs. My dad is standing at the top of the stairs on the landing, hammer in hand, and through the dusty air I see his face red with anger.

'Get here now, Boy!' he screams at me.

Charlotte and I were only having a bit of playful fun; a harmless sibling argument. As I make my way up the stairs towards the landing, he begins shouting down at me and I feel his warm spit landing upon my face.

Once at the top, with the flight of stairs to my rear, he towers over me, shouting while holding the hammer in his hand. He swings it towards my head and stops just before it makes contact with my skull.

My balance is wavering and I'm terrified I might fall backwards. I cower, ducking my head, and hope he'll stop soon. I don't know what the lesson is but I've learned to be smaller and I just want this to stop.

'Look at me, Boy!' he screams. I lift my gaze to behold the sight of dull iron hurtling towards my face. 'Don't you dare be a sissy, squealing to your mother! Man up!'

I cower again, hoping my hands can provide some sort of protection, but, as before, nothing strikes me. My father is now bored of me. He turns away with his back to me. My lesson has been delivered, he has finished shouting – for now.

77

I run away downstairs, with tears in my eyes. I was just playing with Charlotte but I could see in his eyes that he hated me.

I'll never be what he wants me to be, nor do I want to become what he wants me to be.

2

OUR INVISIBLE LIVES

'There are forms of oppression and domination
which become invisible – the new normal.'

Michel Foucault

As we both sat in different rooms of the Spalding police station, with the sun streaming down through the high windows above us, we tried to stretch our weary minds from the terrifying present into the even more terrifying past.

In our respective rooms, our fatigued eyes gazing into the distance and weighed down by the heat and glare, we began to recount our lives to the police family liaison officers. We tentatively sipped water from plastic cups as the grief dried our mouths into sandpaper.

The stuffy, dusty rooms began to disappear as we replayed our lives in our minds. As the bright sun melted the present moment away, we found ourselves back together with our mother and sister, as young boys, carefree and adventurous.

Childhood

Our memories began in a large farmhouse in rural Cambridgeshire. Before this, we had lived briefly in a small townhouse in the town of March, until Luke had a life-threatening allergic reaction to nuts at about the age of three. We were told that our father decided that it would be safer for Luke if we grew our own food and so we moved into a run-down farmhouse in literally the middle of nowhere, with Mum growing the family's food on a vegetable plot.

We lived in a caravan on the driveway for a year because the farmhouse was in such a degenerated condition. The carpets were inches high and knotted together with congealed cat urine. Most of the house was in disrepair and the garden and fields were overgrown with grass that towered past our waists. At one point we discovered an entire bike there, but it took us nearly an hour to unravel the undergrowth that it had become entangled with.

As children, we spent much of our time outside, climbing trees and playing with the family animals: dogs, pigs, chickens, sheep, geese and many more. We lived quite a distance from the village so much of our time was spent together: just us, our combined imaginations and nature to keep ourselves occupied in the vast expanse.

A twelve-year-old Luke articulated this life clumsily and flamboyantly in extracts taken from an autobiography for a school assignment. Charlotte had kept this stored away because it always made her giggle:

Gravel on the Brain

I was about four and Ryan was only three and it was a warm summer's day in about May sometime. All the birds were out singing and the flowers blooming. It smelt like a perfect day. Boom! Bang! There were loud tools being used in the distant background. It totally ruined the summer's effect.

Chirp. Bang! Chirp. Bang! Our house was being tampered with and titivated (well, being built actually) and we were living in a caravan on the drive temporarily until the house was built. It was a new caravan but smelt faintly of sawdust and stuffy, normal caravan disappointments.

Meanwhile, inside Ryan and I were getting agitated by the heat and were having a fight (nothing new there) when he hit me in the stomach. I turned to my left and saw a plasterboard wall, then to my right and spotted a fruit bowl. I jerked my hand down as quick as lightning, picked up a banana and yelled, 'I'm gonna shoot you!'

Ryan span around and sped all around the caravan desperately until he came to the exit door. Since it was a caravan it had those weird steps that go down either side of the door. Yet, Ryan just ran straight forwards, fell off the stairs and got a piece of gravel stuck in his forehead. He let out a loud shriek.

Mum came rushing to the scene. She noticed the gravel stuck in his forehead. She held our hands and threw us into the back of the car. We went toddling off to the hospital and Ryan had to wear these sticky-tape things on his cut. They looked really stupid. I laughed at him every time I saw him. He wanted vengeance.

AAWWW! Vengeance hurts. Quit it!

Approximately one week later, when Ryan's sticky-tape things were removed from his head, he was ready to go on the offensive.

I run around the house to get to places (especially fast to the toilet). It was . . . let me see . . . around nine in the morning because Ryan was having breakfast in the kitchen. Suddenly, as quick as the Road Runner, there were a series of thuds from upstairs, down the stairs, past the living room and, in a flash, I was into the kitchen where Ryan was prowling.

He was waiting for me to come past so he tipped a whole bottle of milk on the floor. I tried to dodge and brake, but my feet slipped across the watery surface and I flew into the air. My head was now my closest body part to the floor. CRASH! My mouth collided with the floor and my two front teeth shattered. Ryan sank his head into his lap and I could hear him sniggering under his breath.

Mum once again came to the scene. This time she didn't seem that surprised. Once again, she grabbed my arm, in the car I hopped and down the road we toddled. I can't remember what happened at the hospital, but I had to wait until I was old enough for my adult teeth to grow before I had any full front teeth. I was really angry this time but sadly didn't get any revenge.

Growing up, our family had always seemed normal enough from an outside perspective. Most of the memories from this part of our life are those of simplicity: being outside, of sunshine and play.

It was a feral childhood for all of us. We spent our days doing whatever caught our fancy, whether it was catching grasshoppers, hiding in the long grass and sneaking up on sheep or simply gazing into the pond and watching the life meandering through the murky waters. Charlotte was several years younger than both of us and nothing astounded us more than watching her grow up. We were fascinated with her tiny hands and feet, her beautiful blonde hair and lively spirit. Despite being younger, she would still play with us at every opportunity. It was in those moments that Charlotte began to develop her powerful affinity with animals. Nature resonated with her and she loved spending all her time with the animals. She was Mother Nature's child. She began horse riding in the fields when she was very young. She stopped after she was injured from a fall but started again some years later: it was to become her favourite pastime.

The land provided us with everything that we needed. It was a straightforward existence. For small children it was the perfect environment. It was a life of nature and of simple pleasures.

However, for as long as we can remember, we always

knew that our father was short-fused. Yet, when we were young this didn't provide us with much concern. We certainly didn't have a problem keeping our distance; we merely bumped into our parents as we ran rampant for days on end. As small children, anger and aggression seemed to be signs of authority; we understood them as instructions that we needed to behave differently. We learned to accept the authority, particularly because we had no other option but also because it seemed pointless to refute it. We had everything that we felt we needed. We grew up simply playing.

Adolescence

We moved to the village of Moulton in 2001, when Luke passed the entrance exams at a nearby grammar school. This new house was far, far smaller than where we had grown up, but it wasn't much different to what we expected for a village house. The previous occupant had been an old lady who had passed away. Again, the carpet was inches thick, almost as if it had grown while no one had tended to it. The wallpaper was nearly as bad; a fluffy texture and a mossy dark-green colour. The air stung our nostrils with the smell of cat urine. To us children, it appeared that we had moved into a damp cave.

Again, we spent many weeks simply knocking things down with sledgehammers. At times, it felt like we had moved there simply to destroy everything.

Despite appearances, renovating this new house was

much more manageable than our previous home; at least this time we didn't have to live in a caravan. However, this didn't stop the sobbing; in many ways it felt as though we had moved out of our childhood.

We'd loved our two dogs at our old house; a Labrador, Bonnie, and a mongrel called Tara. We'd had to give up all the animals when we moved, and it had been difficult to see them go.

Twelve-year-old Luke also commented on this stage of our lives in his autobiography:

The Most Important Move of My Life

In my life I have lived in three different houses. The first was a house in March. It was a normal detached house with an average-sized garden. We lived there until I was three years of age and within those three years I had only two friends who lived within walking distance of our house. We moved from this house because our parents believed that we would have a more comfortable and safe life in the country.

Our second house was enormous with a three-acre garden to run and play in which provided us with hours of fun. It was a five-bedroom house and had a double garage and a driveway big enough to park thirty cars on. We did have one friend, but he lived one and a half miles away and it took us ten minutes to go and see him on a bike. The school was two miles away.

Then in the summer holidays of 2001 we decided to move and ended up at Moulton. We now have over fifteen friends to play with who live within five minutes' walking distance from our new home. We have yet to spend our first full summer here as we moved on August 27th, 2001.

Was it really that good in the beginning? Well, no, to be honest because it was emotionally stressful for all of us. First of all, the week before we moved was spent keeping the old house really, really tidy (which was an enormous challenge for me). Another thing that got at us all was having to send our two old dogs to a dog shelter. Over the many years we had spent living there, we grew to love them. Then, all of a sudden, we had to leave them to go to a new place that me, my brother and my sister didn't want to go to. When we heard our parents say they were putting an offer on this run-down house it nearly made me cry. We looked at each other and opened our mouths as wide as a wormhole - what did they see in this house? Would you buy that house? Definitely not me.

For the next six weeks we lived in complete .and utter horror until we discovered that other children lived around the lane. This really boosted our morale and helped by keeping us away from the house for a long time while our parents 'titivated it' as they said or as I said, 'built it again'.

Anyway, by spring the next year, the 'rebuilding' had been completed and the house looked fine (not great but it was good enough to live in). The next priority was to replant the garden and remove a few trees.

We had replaced the cat-pee-soaked floorboards upstairs, split the upstairs bedroom into two so my brother and I had our own rooms, redid the other bedrooms and bathrooms and finally started on the kitchen.

We were still sad at losing our two dogs. So, I suggested, 'Why not get a dog?' We spent over four weeks looking for a Yorkshire terrier for our family. When we found one in the Yellow Pages, we went to the house to see him. When we arrived, we were taken straight to the puppies. On the way we passed a parrot that kept repeating, 'Hello Max, who's a good boy now?' Once we had a new puppy, we had to choose a name. I was the first to suggest, 'How about Max? That's what the parrot wants to call him.' No one else contributed a name so we went along with that. He looked so cute and we all loved him. He was a shy dog, so it took him a few weeks to get used to us but after that he was happy. So, after all of that we all decided that we liked the house and our new dog.

At first, we were all very shy. We saw some children our age running around outside, and our first reaction was to dive onto the floor and hide. We were almost *Jungle Book* children at this stage of our lives, as most of our socialising outside of school had been with each other and animals. We didn't know how to navigate this world where other people seemed to be running around in what used to be our back garden. We'd never really learned how to approach other people. We only communicated with play.

It didn't take long until the local kids saw that some new people had moved in and began knocking at the door. It was common for a group of kids, sometimes ten or more, to be at the door with the question, 'Are you coming out?'

Before we knew it, we had begun to spill out into the streets and parks and it felt like we'd never lost the space that we had in our old life. In fact, we'd gained many new friends. Our playful lives felt very much the same again.

We hadn't needed money at our last house as we provided for ourselves. Neither of our parents had worked for a decade while we lived there. We had lived an entirely self-sustained lifestyle and produced everything that we needed. The reality of our new situation required both of our parents to work. In our new arrangement our mother worked as much as her multiple sclerosis allowed. Meanwhile, our father worked as little as he could get away with. Mum quickly found work at the local supermarket but our father stuttered. He flitted between jobs and throughout he seemed to become more querulous and aggressive towards us, his family. Eventually, he settled on a job at a local builders' merchant.

This meant our family earned very little with both of our parents working part-time on minimum wage. We always managed though. We spent everything that we had on bills and food. We managed a few family holidays during our childhood; however, these were only the result of a small inheritance or an unexpected pay-out. As children, this didn't concern us at all. We found our enjoyment in nature and learning; both of which were free and abundant. We never desired anything except the things that we had just outside of our door, which were available to all.

As we began to grow into our new environment, our father seemed to be losing control of his temper over entirely irrelevant things for apparently contrived reasons. If the bins needed taking out, this would ruin his entire day as he descended into incoherent grumbles and moans. His world would fixate on that moment and only the new day would distract him from it, at which point he would fixate his frustrations on something else.

He behaved like an impertinent child; if we had behaved the same we'd have expected to be severely reprimanded. He seemed to be purposely creating self-sustaining emotional traps for himself. We created the calmest and most pleasant environment that we could for him, even though it was clear that there was no real reason for his distress. We assumed that he was not adjusting as readily as the rest of us and would acclimatise with time.

These behaviours didn't strike us as unfamiliar. Our father had always seemed to be reactive, like a simple animal. However, it seemed that his anger was becoming more frequent or at least we found it harder to escape. Ordinary life now trapped him in a constant loop of anger. He would repeat himself indefinitely over something as trivial as the fact that the kettle hadn't been filled up. He never realised the futility of his behaviour or intervened in his own distress; he always let it conquer him.

Eventually, our father's initially undirected anger turned to incoherent and unjust blame, now firmly targeted towards all of us. It didn't take long for us to realise that this wasn't simply a transition. What seemed like our father's emotional incompetence was a much larger issue than we had realised, and he planned to condemn us. He became more uneasy as we grew older and began to assume our own responsibilities, plans and ambitions. He seemed to be uncomfortable with us having friends and our mother having work for the first time in a decade. He began to resist the development of every aspect of our lives. Oddly, our father drove our move to the village of Moulton against the rest of our family's wishes, yet now that we were here and we all began to enjoy it, he became increasingly hostile and discontented.

Throughout our childhood, we never remember our father being involved. He never came to a single parents' evening at school and he rarely came to any school sports events. He turned up when we both graduated from university, but that is all we can honestly remember. He was an armchair father. He didn't ever get involved in our day-to-day living except to hinder it and find reasons why we couldn't do things. The only times he got involved in our childhood were either when he saw an opportunity to see us fail and suffer, or to take credit for our achievements and elevate his perceived reputation among the community and family friends. Contradictions never concerned him. He wanted us to fail so he could feel better about himself and yet would also accept the odd success to keep his reputation buoyant. Those triumphs were never allowed to build our self-confidence: he wanted to make sure we had to rely on him.

We became numb to what were now frequent vitriolic outbursts. These seemed arbitrary and random, but we did our best to try to prevent them from arising. The most difficult part was seeing each other suffer; we had all learned to bear our own suffering.

We were slowly conditioned not to do the things that attracted condemnation so as to protect each other from his rages: using fuel to visit friends, performing extra-curricular activities or sports, spending money on anything, having the heating on, any mess – even his – effectively whatever occurred to him at that moment. These restrictions on our lives evolved through a persistent and insidious gradualism. He would complain when we did anything that didn't involve him, but then would never want to do anything at all. This meant that we were gradually restricted until we rarely left the house. We always had to be within his sight.

Our father would often threaten our dogs to force us to concede to his behaviour. In a rage, he would attempt to feed them food that was poisonous to dogs while angrily protesting his ignorance. He would kick them, enforce unnecessarily stringent rules on them or simply yell at them. This was just another way in which he forced us all to concede by attacking us via proxy.

Even as we continued to restrict ourselves in an attempt to reduce his aggression towards us, it only increased. He always found something to complain about no matter what we did. The ordinary father–child, husband–wife relationships had become an ever-constricting vice which would continue until all life and resources had been squeezed out of us.

Despite his behaviour, he condemned us when he was forced to confront his aggression. He wanted us to be his slaves, but he didn't ever want to be cognisant that he had demanded this.

We were all very successful at school and later at sport in spite of this. Our successes simply reinforced the idea that we were living an ordinary life. In giving our father the benefit of the doubt, we had assumed that he couldn't have hindered us that much. He was only yelling at us. He wasn't actually hitting us. We couldn't imagine putting a believable sentence together to explain it or articulate the impact of the aggregation of his behaviours. As we grew older, it became clear that many adults could be particularly unpleasant and that this was possibly just how things were.

Since we weren't failing at school and we didn't have behavioural problems, our situation didn't appear to be something that anyone could help us with. We were looking for signs of violence or our own failures to identify that something was wrong. That didn't happen, so we didn't recognise our suffering or that our father was dangerous. From the outside, we were three healthy, intelligent children. No one seemed concerned that much was wrong, because we were doing so well. In fact, we never broke rules, never asked questions and we were quiet and diligent. However, from the lens of coercive control, these are exactly the symptoms of systematic control, not necessarily the ideal students that these characteristics might suggest.

In contrast to the man we experienced at home, our father's behaviour seemed to be excessively friendly outside of our family. It certainly wasn't anything that we were used to experiencing. He would laugh and bound around with energy, making jokes, seeming light-hearted. Seeing him like this scared us because we knew the duplicity. We heard the cackle in his laugh. We knew the emotional exhaustion of him performing this play would likely leave us bearing the fallout later. Our father had no life outside of the family and simply treated social occasions with a reluctant air of duty, albeit well performed. Due to this, we very rarely had people over to our house. In fact, we tried not to have friends because of the expectation to reciprocate invites and have friends visit.

We began to hide our home life so as not to get others caught up in it and because we were ashamed of our father. We became so used to the duplicity of our father that we believed that all families were like ours. If they seemed happy, it was simply because they were pretending. They were on show, just like we were, like everyone was. We truly believed that all families were fundamentally like ours at home when no one was looking.

Outsiders often described our father as 'protective'. He seemed to be invested in our lives but in reality he was always monitoring and enforcing boundaries. For example, we often couldn't leave the house unless he approved; he insisted on driving us every time we were permitted to leave; and he ran our bank accounts, meaning we always had to ask for money. Any 'protection' that our father gave was simply for him to maintain control under a thin veil of inarticulate, malevolent paternalism. He would never let us remain independent and 'protect' ourselves. Any external appearance of freedom was simply us exhibiting conditioned behaviours, a carefully drilled march that we all knew our places within.

As we grew up, our father's repressive nature became more obvious as we did more to try to become independent. He became like a bored prison guard. He denied our mother's freedom more strongly by preventing her access to a mobile phone and social media. Once we had left for university, we had to call our father and ask to be put through to Mum.

Our mother's MS was regularly triggered by our father's erratic behaviour, where her trigeminal neuralgia would cause her severe facial pain for up to an hour. She was on the strongest painkillers she could possibly be prescribed, yet still the pain tore through and she would be in tears and unbearable agony. Our father would relish the opportunity to use this against us: it allowed him to cause our mother excruciating physical pain and cause us vicarious emotional distress without physical violence. The more pain that our father could cause our mother, the more he would restrict her access to her own money, while claiming that he was saving it up for her MS treatment.

Outside of physical pain, if our mother tried to meet friends from work, our father would accuse her of homosexual activities or of having an affair, simply because his emotional state justified it to him. He would guilt-trip her for weeks for spending £3 on a cup of coffee until she preemptively cancelled plans because the misery he created outweighed any enjoyment she could hope for. She had wanted to travel around Europe with us, but our father hid her passport from her. He refused to let her visit Ryan when he competed in a triathlon representing Great Britain in Turkey, even though the only reason Ryan had entered and trained for it was so that Mum could have a holiday.

Despite restricting our mother's life, our father simply spent his days in the corner of the room on his laptop. His primary concern seemed to be to drag others down rather than to attempt to live his own life.

His life appeared to be some kind of escapism. He hid in the world behind the screen. His only friends were those he had encountered in a chatroom somewhere. He had the desperate naivety of a lonely child in this inter-net universe. Slowly his entire world became imaginary. He believed he knew these people inside out; he believed that they were his soulmates. He once gave thousands of pounds, which he had siphoned from our mother over many years, to someone on the internet with whom he had only exchanged a couple of messages. This person claimed to be a student requesting help to pay off his student loan. Yet, our father was never interested in supporting any of his own children.

Our father would demand more and more from us in the real world as he did less and less. We often tried to coax him away from the computer but were only met with anger for our apparent rudeness. As he became more immersed in this internet world that he had constructed, he decided that he was the voice of objective truth. He demoted us to idiots. He became more interested in conspiracy theories and was frustrated at how little interest we appeared to take in this. He no longer believed any information that was peer-reviewed or scientific, instead perceiving that this was somehow censored. However, he believed without reserve any opinion on an unregulated forum. He forced his political views on us as he became more 'anti-gov' in his abstract paranoia. He drew an ideological line around himself and he discovered that we were on the other side. We were perceived as the enemy of his strange world.

Much of his control over us was never clear to us, until one day we realised an entire domain of life was completely off limits, whether it was our social lives, hobbies or financial independence. Initially, what felt like uneasy compromises to avoid escalation of his bad moods aggregated and we were imprisoned within a structure of his narratives and aggression. He would exert his coercion and control incrementally, often without it ever being clear exactly at which moment we'd been captured. He did whatever he could so as not to raise our alarm. If we became aware that our father was yet again restricting another element of our lives, he would promise that it wouldn't happen again. Yet, it always did. Eventually all the past instances of unreasonable behaviour blurred together, leaving us without the ability to identify the severity of our situation.

One simple example was regarding Ryan keeping his road bike in the living room for easy access, as he cycled almost daily. Our father's bike was never used and so was stored in the garden shed. Suddenly, one day our father insisted on having his own bike in the house, despite him never riding it. He moved Ryan's bike out and put his bike there in its place. Our father saw Ryan as having privileges which, regardless of practicality, had to be revoked. The bicycle placements had never caused any issues; our father had merely one day spotted a new opportunity to restrict us and remind us of his dominance.

It is now clear that those who wish to maintain control will not risk raising the alarm and getting sent to prison. This would give their captives a breath of freedom that they are not willing to risk as well as revealing their behaviour to the world. Our father demanded compromises from us but was never willing to compromise himself. He demanded control but would never be subject to anyone else's rules, let alone his own.

His financial control kept our family poor so that we couldn't survive away from him. He gambled online, wasting the tiny amounts of money that we had on investments that he didn't understand – presumably to force us to stay around if we ever wanted to see the money again. He would even go on holidays by himself, such as a trip to Niagara Falls or Spain. Yet, he deemed the family dogs' obedience training which was one of Charlotte's main hobbies, at £10 once a week, too expensive and cancelled it. He decided entirely how our money was to be spent and rationed out only the bare minimum to our mother for purchasing essentials like groceries. This forced us all to give up even the smallest luxuries. Money spent travelling to a hobby would be recorded and he would attempt to inflict guilt on us by insisting that this was preventing us from being able to feed ourselves. Even buying food was targeted, although it's not clear what he expected us to do outside of fasting, especially considering that he would forever complain that our mother's cooking was never good enough.

This behaviour forced us to live secret lives and conceal the most basic expenditure to purchase staple goods. He allowed himself to complain at either end of any spectrum and bemoan our moderation. He would have no difficulty complaining about our flawless execution of his authoritarian instructions, blaming us for carrying out the very action he insisted upon. He feasted on his own self-pity and self-righteousness.

He simply wanted to create a world in which we were fearful to do anything at all and withdrew into exhausted and confused submission, drowned in annihilated self-esteem and passivity.

We had to lie to make this life work. He had created a world that it was only possible for us to live in through contradictions. He wanted to create a system whereby we were always in the wrong and he could elevate himself through his distribution of blame and dissatisfaction with all that we did.

We frequently attempted to approach him to get help, believing that our father was 'mentally ill'. However, he only saw this as threatening – us conspiring against him – and a further challenge to his power. After we continued to pursue the issue, despite his explosive bouts of indignation, he would simply regress into a pitiful child. He would entirely withdraw and became a useless, helpless baby. He would expect us to do everything for him while he built his strength up for his next histrionic outburst.

When life didn't follow his naive, narcissistic plan, our father was always the unfortunate victim: the immoral world had conspired to ruin him. He was somehow always the perfect victim. Everything was a targeted act in a world that singled him out. His resentfulness and bitterness were his defining characteristics.

He was hostile and jealous if we demonstrated any gratification at all to our mother. When others were struggling, he disregarded their suffering jealously. Like an entitled child, everything had to be about him, or it wasn't permitted. When others were suffering he believed this was an affront to his power and an attempt to divert attention away from him.

A further deterioration in his behaviour occurred after he was diagnosed with prostate cancer. He went through the necessary procedures and the cancer was removed in a standard operation. However, it didn't seem to leave him at all; instead it festered in his mind. It became the next layer to his obsessions. He became fixated upon stress. He blamed stress for the prostate cancer and inevitably he blamed us for the stress. He began to form dogmatic routines to reassure or delude himself of his insecurities.

For example, he insisted on drinking green tea every day. If anything prevented this routine, we would incur his rage. He even produced thousands of pages in a secret diary documenting his levels of stress, how much we had annoyed him that day and that he hadn't been for a walk because he had simply sat at his laptop all day again. He expected us to manage his health and wellbeing for him; it was our responsibility to schedule and invite him out for walks. Often he would refuse because we picked a bad time, and still blame us in his diary for his lack of exercise that day. He blamed us for even the most trivial failures in his life. Often, we would find our only available money had been spent on an industrial-sized bag of seeds that possessed some anti-oxidants, a smoothie maker or an exercise bike. None of these were ever used.

Despite his obsessive concern about himself, he had no respect for any of us. In our early teens, our mother revealed to us all at dinner that she had cancer. Our father immediately launched into a tirade where he blamed all of us for stressing him out with the situation, potentially worsening his prostate cancer (which he didn't have any more). He screamed at us because none of us understood what it was like for him that *his wife* had cancer. His behaviour was laughable: there was no clear rational starting point to address it.

Over the years, as we grew closer to our mother, our father withdrew even more. He became angry and paranoid that his children weren't 'like' him, believing we were conspiring against him. We never understood why our father was so dominating, or why he was determined to make his entire world one full of misery. Why would he choose to build and force such a miserable life onto himself and others? Whenever we tried to leave, he made arbitrary threats. He said he would make things up to get us all sent to prison. He said he'd burn the house down.

'Worse things will happen – don't you dare!'

Despite only showing us hatred, we still had sympathy for what we perceived was weakness. How could someone so weak be dangerous? We would try to offer our advice – however, he never wanted it. He simply wanted to attack us. He wanted us to feel the same pain that he had concocted within himself. He couldn't understand why we weren't as angry and despairing as he was, so he looked to selfishly and jealously inflict it upon us.

Even in the rare event that he came back from work happy, he would force us to laugh and join in. He would furiously demand that we mirrored him, whatever mood he was in. He was incapable of letting us live our own lives. In fact, he wouldn't let any of us have time together and would often turn up unannounced in different rooms in the house, leaving his sacred spot in the living room, to try to 'catch us out'.

Our father was not physically abusive in the stereotypical caricature of an abuser that we held in our minds. He didn't consider his actions to be wrong, either. In his murder note he wrote, 'yes, we bickered, but it wasn't serious,' claiming 'it was normal marriage stuff. No violence.' He then proceeded to act in exactly that way.

The broken beliefs that our father aggressively held about being a father and a husband simply meant that we had to take up the roles that he had failed to perform. Even after his familial role had descended into redundancy, he continued to cling to his views. As we grew older and began to develop our own moral understanding, we challenged our father more frequently and powerfully. This only made our situation worse. He was only interested in his own interpretation of his life. He wasn't willing to let reality interfere with that. Our father had successfully created a world in which we had no option other than to confine ourselves to his prison. After a while, his words and actions crept into our minds, disabling our ability to fight back. With each infraction, the prison bars closed in further.

Everything that he condemned in the world was really an aspect of himself. He would transparently project his own self-hatred onto others. It was so poorly masked as to be embarrassing. He would accuse Ryan of being a sociopath because of his loving and caring behaviour. Our father's language was simply contradictory. Where he saw love, he recoiled and attacked it as hate.

At times, we believed that his behaviour was getting better. The truth was that we had in fact conceded yet further and learned to expect less from him. By remaining inconsistent yet forceful, he unsettled any self-belief and we were often in serious doubt about our own judgements. By destroying our interpretation of events, we were paralysed into inaction. Since our father was interested in total control, it is now clear why he was unlikely to simply dish out a few bruises that might have gotten him caught. He was not as instinctive as we believed him to be: his behaviour was carefully and cold-heartedly calculated.

Since the deaths of Mum and Charlotte, we now understand that our experience was not unique; it shared many common threads with the experiences of others. We've come to realise that what we had perceived as a lack of control or 'mental illness' in our father was the clinical application of anger as a tool to coerce us. Emotion was the excuse.

Where we had previously seen arrogance and aggression as a sign of authority, we began to see that it was simply the pitiful consequence of weak-mindedness.

Our father was incredibly unpleasant but had done nothing to produce any evidence that could allow us to protect ourselves from him. We had to learn to channel our thoughts and sublimate our emotions as necessary in order to carry on. There was no immediate way that we could resolve this. We had to plan for a different future. We were propelled by fear, but if we could concentrate on bettering ourselves then maybe one day we could raise enough money to get out of this situation.

Despite our successes, in many ways we always believed that we were part of the problem. We couldn't meet the brutally enforced rules and circumstances of our lives. Whatever we did we could not make our lives pleasant. We were too lazy, too unintelligent, too selfish to be able to meet the requirements set out for us. We were bad kids.

Where every other avenue was cut off, we just got on with life and whatever happened to be in front of us rather than giving up. After all, it's always possible to find a million reasons to give up. We had to find one to carry on.

Flashback – Birthday Blues

RYAN

'. . . *Happy birthday, dear Ryan. Happy birthday to you!*'

I hate birthdays, especially my own. Birthdays usually mean extra attention and often a forced and excruciating family day out, forced to look as if I am enjoying myself:

smiling, as pain streams from my eyes, and attempting to perform exactly as my father expects. Birthdays are to be endured, not enjoyed. Birthdays are just more arbitrary rules that have to be obeyed.

'Why is this taking so long?! You stupid boy!'

Our father berates each of us as he stands at the door, having collected the car keys. He watches and moans, ordering us to hurry. Yet, he does nothing himself as we run around shutting the windows and locking the doors.

'Hurry up! We're going to be bloody late!'

The environment at home is always constricting. We suffer from claustrophobia, not of space but of time, emotions and autonomy. Every human instinct must be crushed to meet our father's impossible expectations. We are responsible for his wellbeing, yet he communicates nothing but rage so we must simply guess what he wants, as if he was a perpetually screaming baby.

Our father always works himself into a fury like this; to an onlooker it would appear short-tempered. However, we know these furies are just his means to enforce command and control. We know his contrived anger is a constant reminder of his control and power. He creates tension and anger to squeeze us into compressed coils of anxiety. Then he can demand 'just do it!', and we spring rapidly into action under his command.

So, here we are. Ready for a journey, showered with rage instead of confetti. It's not often we get a birthday trip, the fuel costs too much – as he always says, 'it's fuel or food'. For whatever reason, he's decided that this has to happen, but frankly none of us want to go out. It's certainly going to be more hassle than if we stayed here, and paradoxically it will almost certainly feel more claustrophobic.

Now he is seething with manufactured rage, we get to look forward to his threatening and erratic driving.

Great, another family trip, our rolling eyes reveal to one another as we step into the car. We're so used to being silenced by him that we understand each other without saying a word. He thinks silence prevents us communicating, but we've been forced to practise it for so long that it has become another language to us.

We drive in absolute silence. Any word out of place and our father is likely to begin yelling at all of us. Our father's face is creased and loaded with seething tension. We're aware he is waiting for an opportunity to target it at us.

'Woman! Is it this turning?' our father suddenly demands.

We're always ready for him to hurl his responsibility onto all of us, propelled by rage. We're always prepared in a state of permanent anxiety so we can respond to his random, erratic and unpredictable demands.

Once again, we need to frantically come up with a solution to make up for our father's incompetence. Our father's mind is awash with uncertainty. He refuses to accept uncertainty in any aspect of life. Rather than continuing to drive ahead, he begins swerving towards exits and changing lanes in an instant. Cars beep and are forced to turn out of our way.

I sense an urge of self-destruction in our father, of wilful recklessness with our lives. An aspect of him wants to turn the car off the road right now, but he's enjoying our fear too much, so he keeps us in this purgatory.

Our mother finds the road we need, and our father dives into the junction and everything calms temporarily. Our father is now laughing, yet we're all shaking. He sees every action of his to be funny and infinitely excusable. Any mistake we make is infinitely punishable. His laughing cuts at us; it shows how different he is to us. It shows how little he respects our lives, emotions or wishes. He only sees us as an extension of him; we don't deserve to respond differently. In fact, it never even occurs to him that we do. He only cares about himself.

Despite these frequently self-inflicted furies, our father always insists on driving. Our mother is never allowed to drive when our father is in the car since 'of course, a woman doesn't drive a man around'.

It's not long until the next incident: 'Where are my sunglasses, Woman? It's too bright!' The same process unfolds again even though he can see fine. He doesn't know where he last put them and he is frustrated that our mother hasn't pre-empted his desire for them.

These incidents populate any family event. Everything that happens to our father is an urgent frustration that needs to be resolved by someone else. He hates us because we haven't anticipated his every need before he is forced to articulate it. Although, it is a stretch to say that he is able to articulate his needs or that meeting his requests gives him any satisfaction. At best, we can only hope to not be a nuisance or to not make things worse. We never seem to add anything to his life.

At last, we have arrived at the restaurant. Whatever happens now, at least we're safe.

'The sun's in my eyes!'

'These seats are no good, my back hurts!'

'I can't fucking eat like this, I'm sweating, open the window!'

'Oi, waiter, are you going to get us our drinks, or what?'

'This is the last time I ever come here!'

They try to bring us a birthday cake, with thirteen candles for me to blow out. My mother organised this small gesture as a kind surprise, but my father refuses it, saying we have one at home. The staff, in a mumbled disorientation, muddle back into the kitchen. In a way, I'm glad this is over.

Thankfully, we eventually arrive home from the miserable trip, but our father's harassment doesn't stop. It's normally worse at home, but it's less embarrassing at least.

'Stop it, Dad! They can't eat that!'

He has proceeded to feed some cake to our dog, protesting ignorance at the fact that the chocolate cake – which our father always chooses – is highly toxic to dogs. I reach out to hold open Max's jaws while removing as much cake as I can. This is a yearly occurrence with birthday cakes and an almost weekly occurrence with other food, yet he continues to act out like this.

This inevitably erupts into an irrational argument again. He is never content when attention is not focused on him; birthdays always cause him to explode with jealousy.

I hate birthday cakes. They cause more pain than they're worth.

I hate birthdays. They cause so many arguments.

Happy birthday, Ryan . . .

Adulthood

After we had moved on to university, our father's behaviour became more unstable. He terrified our mother and Charlotte.

We had always accepted that our life wasn't anywhere near perfect; in fact, most of the time it was utterly exhausting. However, the entire time we were all looking out to make sure his anger didn't become physical. This was our benchmark to determine if he had changed from unpleasant to dangerous. At that point we would run with whatever we had, but he knew this and carefully managed his behaviour just enough to grind us down but not enough to force us to flee into poverty.

So, we endured, and so our father continued for many years. He was always perplexed as to why his family seemed to be drifting further from him. He always failed to take a different perspective. He always resorted to the same aggressive tactics to both push us away and force us to stay. He remained intransigent. He realised that we were all children of our mother and saw how different he was to all of us. This only aggravated him further. Nothing he could do could shape us in his image. He was the image of what we refused to become.

As we left university and began earning money, our father became more jealous and aggressive. It appeared that he knew his position was fragile, even if he wouldn't consciously admit it to himself. His enforced poverty would soon no longer restrict the lives of our mother and sister as we could provide for them.

He must have known that his behaviour was unacceptable, and that infinitely squeezing us would eventually make it impossible for us to stay. However, he never addressed any of those issues directly. Instead his entitled anger spilled out everywhere.

Now that we were able to provide for our mother and sister, he saw us as both competition and a source of financial income. He would charge us £20 per night to visit home, saying it was our mother who was demanding this money for food (which was untrue). Objecting to his request would have just incurred his anger and rage. He tried to waste our money – he insisted Ryan pay £10,000 for renovating the garage and installing an unnecessary electric garage door for Ryan's motorbike. When Ryan refused, our father descended into rage. He made countless and frequent requests for money or expensive items, trying to convince us that it was our mother making these demands or that it was in our best interests to buy them for him. In his mind the money we earned, just like our mother's wages, all belonged to him.

As we continued to send money home, it did nothing to relieve the financial stress on our family. In fact, it made our father more selfish. It became clearer that he only wanted problems and that no amount of money would alleviate the poverty he cultivated at home through his wastefulness. He even prevented our mother taking on more work as he refused to allow her to bring home more money than him, even though she was not allowed access to it.

Our father seemed to require regular emotional attacks on us to keep his self-opinion buoyant. He had to reassure himself about his insecurities by bringing us down. This gave him the necessary feelings of superiority and the endorphin rush from our suffering. His attacks were so clearly about him and not us. His favourite was to scream how stupid we were: we were top students. There were many available insults that would have been legitimate, but he was not interested in those: he was only interested in holding us accountable for his own insecurities.

Despite his behaviour, our father would complain that no one understood him. This was not surprising because he made no effort to understand anyone else. Every area of his life was always chaotic, yet he never failed to condemn everyone else or to assume any responsibility.

He would continually pivot and contradict himself to always appear to be in the right, at least to himself. With time, that required more and more lies and anger.

We learned to live in spite of our father. At times, we simply rolled our eyes as he would scream at us for hours, storming around the house, slamming doors and repeating himself until he burned out. In a conflict, most people back down when they see that the other side has yielded. Our father would gain momentum, and like a beast with a taste for blood, he would go even harder. To mitigate this, we learned to separate our internal state from our external appearance. We learned to generate a stoic poker face that we wore throughout our lives, no matter what we were going through.

As a family it seemed that we had nothing to contribute to our father's life. We only served as yet another potential obstruction, persistently overwhelming him with stress in what he perceived were carefully orchestrated attacks. He seemed to have no desire to intervene in his emotional state; he utilised it as a tool against us. Whichever way the winds of his life blew him, he would tumble down his carefully constructed emotional mountain, endlessly picking up momentum. All we could do was jump out of the way.

Since he was ungrateful for everything, we were simply better off not doing anything. He would often screw his face up and huff and grumble increasingly until it became so unbearable that we had to ask the inevitable question: 'What is it?' That gave him the justification to blow.

Our father interacted with us as if we were his slaves. We only deserved to exist if we were useful to him. Our restricted resources made this our reality. We simply had to get our heads down and attempt to fund an escape.

After Ryan had started his new job in Holland, the escape plan started to take shape. In June 2016, our mother told our father she was going to leave him; she demanded that the house be put up for sale. The three main chains our father had maintained for the previous twenty-five years – financial control, dependency through us children and isolation – had broken and no longer imprisoned our mother; freedom was no longer just a fantasy, it was a possibility. Despite being clear that she wanted to go, our father refused to accept reality and he attempted a manipulative reconciliation. He coerced our mother into declaring that they were only downsizing. Our father's behaviour was frightening, and so our mother realised she had to pretend to go along with his plans for fear of what he might do.

Our father believed he had kept his coercive behaviour

hidden from the outside world. He clung desperately to his reputation with the neighbours as a perfect father, with a perfectly functioning family. However, much to his displeasure, we had bought Mum a smartphone for Christmas, which meant she could begin to collate evidence of his behaviour which we could show to the rest of the world if and when we needed. In addition to this, for some months our mother had been keeping a diary of everything our father had said and done; however, she still didn't feel that she could take it to the police because there had been no physical harm.

Our father was intensely uncomfortable with Mum possessing a phone and would steal it and ring numbers in the middle of the night to find out who picked up. The freedom this phone enabled her led to our father's escalating suspicion and demands for oversight of what was going on in her digital world. He would often loiter furtively at the supermarket just to check that our mother was at work.

After the 2008 financial crisis in the UK, our father had become paranoid about banks. Our family's £15,000 of life savings was stored in a hidden compartment in a wardrobe. To be able to support our mother and sister, we needed half of those savings to add to our own. If our father had been able to downsize the family home, he would have been able to dispose of the liquidated value, therefore preventing our mother from ever leaving him.

So, our mother took her half of the family savings. Our father was furious the very next day, indicating that he had been checking the savings every day for nearly a decade. Shortly afterwards, our mother was coerced into handing back her half of the money and our father imme-diately took the day off work. He withdrew every penny from the online bank account, took all the cash from the house and from our mother's purse and disappeared. He returned unannounced a few days later and attempted to make amends by returning the money, including Mum's half of the savings.

Our father then purchased a safe and insisted our mother place her half into it. At this point, we had signed a rental contract for our mother and Charlotte to move into their new home on Thursday 14 July. To stall him long enough, our mother had said that her half of the cash was stored at work and promised it would be back on the 14th when she returned home.

However, on the 13th, our father woke in the middle of the night, locked all the doors and locked our mother's passport in the safe. He took all the keys, including the house and car keys, and hid them in the house. When Mum woke up the next morning and confronted our father, he claimed to have lost the keys, even though they had always been kept in the same place for years. He then insisted that he drive her to work so that he could ensure he collected her and the money that evening. We collected our mother from work that morning and broke her free of the house by lunchtime.

Coercive control is understood as the pathological pattern of behaviours designed to reduce the autonomy, resources and self-esteem of its victims. Its very invisibility comes from the abuser exploiting the frequency of abusive behaviour over the visual significance of any individual event. The victim's resulting trauma is the effect of the aggregation of abuse. Coercive control is designed to live in the psychological realm for the very reason that it cannot be seen.

Coercive control is designed to isolate and silence its victims, but even those who do speak struggle against the limited capacity of words to truly describe an environment that is cultivated over years. The oppressive environment felt by the abused family is invisible to a temporary observer.

It is not possible to truly capture coercive control by examples; it's necessary to understand the options that the victims face. The trauma from coercive control is derived not from what is done, but from the constant realisations by the victims of what cannot be done; it is the avenues the abuse has severed. The true losses from coercive control are the options that were never available; the paths that were never taken and the lives that were silently stolen.

Coercive control is the isolation created by invisible chains. It is the strangling silence where others demand evidence of 'a significant event' rather than understanding the effects of the accumulation of abuse. Currently the severity of coercive control is judged from the perspective of the abuse given and not the perspective of the abuse suffered.

Coercive control is where the system that is lived under is itself dangerous. Coercive control is strategic abuse.

Our father's unyielding masculine-fundamentalist belief system was central to how he treated his family. He was coldly manipulative; emotion was simply a tool that he leveraged to burden and intimidate us. Fundamentally, he felt entitled to direct these aggressive emotional states towards us.

Our father struggled to maintain control and relevance as the rest of us strived to grow more independent. He felt he had to justify his position at the top of the household by creating fear to reduce us to dependence. When we adapted and provided for ourselves, his control collapsed and he turned on us.

Gender violence and psychological abuse are a product of the entitlement that comes from a misogynistic and patriarchal belief system. Our father believed that he deserved special treatment and excessive resources purely because of his ideological position as father. This entitlement demands subjugation of women and children, simply for the patriarch to remain at the top. This is the true cause of men enforcing misery, control and murder on their families.

Everything that happened to our father, he chose to do to himself. Every possible way out, he shut the door in front of him. Our father assumed that every action we took was an attack on his manhood and he reacted belligerently. Any event in life became a stimulus and he became the aggressive reaction.

It is only now that we so clearly see the danger of such a rigid patriarchal belief system. The development of our father's psychological abuse occurred slowly enough that our ordinary responses of resilience blinded us to the danger that we were in. We had experienced his behaviour for so long that we didn't believe a different world was possible.

We had never understood him because we rationalised his perspective from our own sympathetic outlook. We had not considered how truly evil he may have been because we were not able to comprehend a mind such as his.

Naturally, we believed that we were somehow protected from the brutal realities of life.

Flashback – Don't Bat an Eyelid

LUKE

'They're for burglars, apparently,' Ryan informs me, sarcastically.

'We've never been burgled though? I'm confused.'

'Mention that and he'll just yell at you.'

'Why all of a sudden though? It's not like our risk of being burgled is now significantly greater.'

There are baseball bats littered around the house in conspicuous locations. Yesterday, our father decided that we needed these. Despite Ryan being six-foot-one at fourteen and me, six-foot-six at fifteen, it appears our father believes we need bats to protect ourselves.

'Even if we did get burgled, there are so many baseball bats, the burglar would find one as soon as he came in. Everyone would end up equipped with a baseball bat, no one would have an advantage.' I'm scratching my head and chuckling.

Ryan laughs, 'He's an idiot. Don't expect it to make sense. That's where you're going wrong.'

'I don't even think there's anything in here worth that much. If I burgled us, I'd probably steal the baseball bats.'

'The funny thing is, you know he won't even let us go outside and play baseball with one of those.'

Ryan's right. We both laugh, shaking our heads, and stare at the bat in the corner of the living room.

'I suppose we'll have to pretend we don't see them. If we even ask why, there'll be hell to pay.'

'See what?' Ryan says and we both laugh, still shaking our heads.

Picking Up the Pieces

As we concluded giving our stories to the police liaison officers, we felt the feelings of anguish and sickness returning. Once again we found ourselves in a world that felt less real than our imagination. How we wished to return to our minds and live there for ever.

In the following days we frequently met with police family liaison officers as they kept us up-to-date with their investigations.

They informed us that our father had been writing drafts of his murder note for months. He had in fact been planning to kill his entire family weeks before we had even planned to move out. He was simply updating his justification each time.

We made many discoveries of our own which began to reveal the true cause of our father's actions. As we were collecting belongings from the family home we found a to-do list that our father had produced in the days running up to the event. It was so coldly ordinary: it included buying a second-hand fridge that he only planned to have for a few days; he even bartered on the sale to save £5 off the listed price. He was functioning perfectly well; nothing had changed in him. After all, he had managed to comfortably write a twelve-page murder note explaining his justifications for killing his family. On 18 July, four days after Mum moved out, our father returned a rental car he had been leasing, on time, to avoid the late fee. He cooked himself a meal he described as his 'last supper' and he'd even purchased a parking ticket on 19 July, minutes before murdering our mother and sister.

This wasn't how we understood murder. There were no examples of a 'loss of control'. In fact, there appeared to be an excess of control.

We began to realise that our father's anger was contrived. It protected him from ever having to reflect on the consequences of his actions; his entitlement assured him soothingly that he was correct. He therefore displayed a total inability to back down when challenged. Any refusal by our family to subordinate to him led to an indefinite escalation until we conceded. It seems that if we had not backed down for all those years, we would have all been killed many years earlier.

Most people have never encountered a murderer and therefore don't know what they're looking for. By the time we learned, it was too late. Our perception of domestic abuse had involved a defunct model of escalating physical attacks, but all the physical violence came at once.

We suddenly understood that it's the clumsy abusers who get caught and inform the stereotype, not the truly dangerous ones who kill their victims before there is a chance for them to speak. We realised the significant danger of those like our father who keep their behaviour below the radar, those who carefully cultivate their control and coercion. Those who appear to others to be *ordinary* men.

Our father's actions demonstrated to us that it doesn't take a loss of control of emotion or mind to kill; in fact, killing is carried out through an act of total control. It is not to be excused on the grounds of 'not being oneself'; killing is the final confirmation of who they are.

We now began to see our father, not as someone who had little control of his emotions, but as someone who had considerable control of them and utilised them to manipulate us.

He did this to consume our lives with the management of his emotion so that we did not have the strength or time for anything else. Whatever we gave, our father would take away. He was a black hole absorbing all our energy. It was never a matter of when he gained control, but how much suffering we had to endure before he got it.

It's now clear that our father had no concern for his character, only his reputation. His reputation merely allowed him the freedom to continue inflicting arbitrary psychological and emotional punishment unchallenged.

The words that he spat out had no meaning to him. He simply used them to turn our own morality and goodness against us until we controlled ourselves. The language of abusers is manipulation; he was not interested in resolving problems, only in feeling right. Someone who demands that they are always right must shape the world around their distortions until it becomes so fragile that it breaks.

As children, it was very easy to believe the reasons we were given for our life. Our father created the circumstances which governed the rationalisations. We did live in relative poverty. He carefully made sure of that. We couldn't afford to see our friends, waste food or take part in extra-curricular activities. Our mother couldn't do anything but clean. But he chose to waste the few resources we had to create this environment, to justify his rage at us. This was normal family life; it was all we'd ever experienced.

Our father had learned to conceal who he really was before we were even born. He carefully controlled every aspect of his external life to prevent the truth from leaking out. It was a case of one lie requiring another until he was in over his head, at which point he brought the entire hole in on the rest of us. He believed that he had the right to behave like this because the only thing that mattered was his opinion of himself and keeping his true nature covered up.

On the day that we broke our mother free from the house, she revealed that our father had been married before he met her. This fact meant very little, but it amazed us how everyone in our life had been sworn to silence by him. It showed how determined he was to conceal facts about himself. He had always been an antagonist to reality. It was revealing to also discover that the apparent reason that he had left his previous wife was because she didn't want children.

When our mother first met our father, he took her contraceptive pills away and insisted, 'You are having my child!' Luke's birth inevitably forced our mother down the road of commitment. Our father always intended to have leverage over a woman and he always intended to use it. Children and poverty would leave her no choice but to remain on the road he had committed her to. Our father also never cared for animals and treated them with disgust – it's clear now that he only reluctantly allowed us to have them because he believed it would make it harder for us to leave.

It is only in the past couple of years that these and other pieces of our childhood have fallen into place. For example, in the process of completing the *Domestic Homicide Review*, it was revealed that our initial move to the countryside was an act of severance. We were told by our father that it was because Luke had a nut allergy and we needed to grow our own food for Luke to be safe. Luke had suffered a serious allergic reaction as a small child and was rushed to hospital to save his life. We were led to believe that this event was a catalyst for our move. However, it transpired that our father knew about Luke's allergy and had fed him nuts regardless in an act of control over our mother. We had moved from our first home not out of concern for Luke, but rather to isolate Mum from her family who lived nearby.

We were also told that our move from the countryside to the village in 2001 was to be nearer to Luke's grammar school, but it emerged that it was to move our mother further again from her family and the friendships she had formed. A lot of people didn't even know we'd left as it was carried out in such a hurry. At the funeral, several old friends asked, 'Where have you been for the last fifteen years?'

Even relationships within our extended family were frequently severed. Our father took our sister out of primary school for a month to go with him and his mother to the wedding of our cousin in Australia. Naturally, our mother wasn't given the option to go as it was her role to housekeep. For the first few days of the holiday, our aunties, uncles, father, grandmother and Charlotte all stayed in a villa near the venue. Our father then had a confrontation with family members over a request for our father to shower before entering the pool. He was so unwilling to compromise that, rather than showering, he took our sister and grandmother away from the villa, forced them to miss the wedding ceremony and banned us children from contacting any of our extended family for close to a decade afterwards.

Contact with them only resumed after our grandmother was diagnosed with dementia and moved into a care home. Our father resumed contact with his sister because he wanted power of attorney over our grandmother's finances and needed his sister's cooperation. Our father could see that our grandmother's house and savings were being used to pay for her care home, and he wanted to do everything in his power to maximise his inheritance. After a few months of attempting to legally gain control of our grandmother's estate, and realising it wasn't possible, he ceased visiting her.

Throughout our lives, there was a silent solidarity

between our mother, Charlotte and the two of us. We chose perseverance which made our situation invisible to the outside world. We couldn't afford to give up because we were responsible for each other's futures.

However, now it is painfully clear that silence hides violence. When we feel like we can't speak about something that is exactly when we need to speak out most urgently. Oppression begins by shaming and coercing us into silence.

Our reality was only articulated to us as we sat in the police station just a couple of days after 19 July. Behind us we saw a poster highlighting coercive control. This poster articulated our father's behaviours exactly. It was the first time we'd heard of the concept of coercive control and discovered that it was a crime. The following characteristics were detailed on the poster:

1. **Isolation from friends/family and restricting an independent social life**

   Every time we had moved to a new house it was an act of purposeful severance of our mother's relationships. Our father had forbidden social media access and controlled our mother's use of the internet. Her daily movements had to follow a strict and regular schedule. He would never clean the house, fill the car with petrol or do any grocery shopping to ensure our mother was busy with chores during her days off work and therefore couldn't spend time with others.

2. **Monitoring activities and movements**

   Daily, our father would look over the phone records

of incoming and outgoing calls. He would call back numbers he didn't recognise. He would be seen at our mother's place of work, hiding behind shelves in the supermarket where she worked.

3. Creating and enforcing arbitrary rules

Our household lived under the domination of ever-changing, illogical rules and unachievable expectations, to which we would all be held strictly accountable, but from which our father was exempt.

4. Threatening reporting to the authorities

Our father would frequently make threats to report us to the authorities for various tax fraud/avoidance crimes we hadn't committed – our father controlled all finances. Our mother's restricted access to the internet meant she had no way of checking whether the threats were credible and, when our father's threats were made against us children, our mother was quick to concede.

5. Controlling finances

Our father had sole access to the family's online accounts. He would scrutinise our mother's credit card spending and ration out the minimum feasible quantity of cash to her. Bills and grocery shopping were all that our mother was permitted to use this money for and even this was a constant source of harassment. Meanwhile, our father would waste large sums of money without justification and refused accountability.

6. Repeatedly belittling and criticising

As victims of abuse, we had grown up believing that we were the problem. Often this was carried out by the aggressive and capricious enforcement of trivial rules, retrospectively applied. These wore us down and left us feeling powerless, useless and hypervigilant as we attempted to predict the arbitrary system governing our lives.

We had never understood how cruel human beings could be. We had not believed that our father could have only wanted a family so that he could dominate us. We were nothing more than expressions of his will to him; we had no right to our own existence or freedom. We were never truly alive under him. Our existence was only conditional.

Flashback – Worked Up

'Yes, Claire is here today,' says Mum's colleague. She puts the phone down. 'That's weird, he hung up again. I think that was your husband, Claire.' Mum's colleague looks awkwardly down to avoid discussing the issue further.

Mum subtly shakes her head, embarrassed.

'Oh never mind, it'll just be about what extra shopping he'd like me to get after work.' Mum musters a faint laugh, but in her eyes there is a flash of hopelessness.

Each call is a threat. He is watching her from his panopticon. At any point, he may check where she is, what she's up to and who she is with.

The phone rings again. Mum's heart drops. Is it him again? The anxiety kicks in.

'Certainly, I'll pass you over to the relevant department,' responds Mum's colleague to the caller.

It wasn't him this time, but does it really make any difference? Any time the phone rings, she fears it is him. Whether it is or not is irrelevant now.

He hadn't needed to check where Mum was, he'd been there all along: inside her head. He is the voice evaluating all of her decisions. She sees her own life through his lens, his interpretation, his desires, his rage.

3

MYTHS OF ABUSE

'He who does not prevent a crime
when he can, encourages it.'

Seneca

DIY and the Virtues of Murderers

Once we had arrived back in Spalding after the murders, the police told us not to read any press coverage of the attack. Luke read nothing for months, but Ryan could only avoid it for a few days. He was shocked to find reports that were sympathetic towards our father. Newspapers quoted locals who described our father as 'a nice guy' and reported that he was 'a DIY nut'. Others even dared to describe him as 'always caring'.

Alongside this, one writer claimed that the murder of our mother and sister was 'understandable'. In every report, there was speculation that the prospect of divorce 'drove' our father to murder. Throughout, there was little mention or description of our mother or sister.

As crimes go, killing your innocent wife and daughter

seemed to us to be as close to objectively bad as it is possible to get. The most heinous crimes are committed by those who should have known or had responsibilities to behave better.

However, it became abundantly clear that the commentary intended to overlook the issue of domestic abuse and failed to draw together the ideological threads between disparate domestic homicides. The treatment of our tragedy was to palm it off as an awkward situation. The responses indicated a wish to do nothing and, in many cases, they were defences of our father's character. No one was willing to admit that this was going to happen again the next week. But, in fact, it would, and does: in England and Wales two women are killed by a current or former partner every single week.[1] In addition, every day almost thirty women attempt suicide as a result of experiencing domestic abuse, and every week three women take their own lives,[2] feeling it is their only way to escape. Yet, after Mum and Charlotte's murders, the police told the public that incidences such as these were 'incredibly rare'.

There was a palpable fear of interfering with our father's central position in the household, even when dead. The dominant belief remained that his home was his business and he had the right to dispense whatever punishments he deemed fit. However, in our case, it was the rest of us who kept our household functioning. Our father was a deadweight who not only weighed us down, but actively pulled us back. We certainly would have been better off without a father. His position in our family was simply ideological.

The myths that we encountered after the murders high-lighted how damaging many of our stereotypes around domestic abuse are. Many of those beliefs perpetuate abuse. To begin with, we were shocked that such irrelevancies as our father's DIY skills could even be mentioned after he chose to murder our family. When someone chooses to kill, they are no longer the person who was good at DIY. They have concluded their life as a killer. No one has the right to use moral accounting to offset arbitrary skills against gross immoral misconduct. No one has the right to simply pick which favourable moment of someone's life defines them and ignore the rest. A killer has defined themselves clearly enough that narratives at this point are not only pointless, but dangerous.

The public and media could not have known how we suffered decades of emotional and psychological torment at the hands of our father. However, it seemed that in the absence of information, there were many who chose the side of a terrorist who committed murder. Should the murders not have clarified the nature of our father and raised questions about the reality of our lives under him?

Even if this escaped observation, the sympathising male angle of the reporting revealed our default societal perspec-tive. Despite what our father had done, some still described him as a 'good man'. We were particularly struck by the use of the word 'always' in the demonstrably incorrect comment that our father was 'always caring'. Who could say this about a murderer and why? To register surprise? There are much more intelligent and constructive ways of indicating surprise after such an event.

Beyond the spattering of irrelevant and incoherent commentary on our father's character, we encountered many recurring arguments in defence of domestic abuse that were wrapped tightly in self-sealing logic. It seemed that victims were not allowed to leave or stay without their actions being disapproved of. These arguments leave victims with nowhere to go and it became clear that this is exactly what they are intending to achieve: to smother victims into silent submission. It was interesting to see replicas of our father's coercive behaviours mimicked on a larger scale, which demonstrated that the beliefs responsible for his actions are prevalent within society.

As we peered further through the commentary on the murders, we observed a fascination with the sawn-off shotgun that our father had used to carry out the murders. During the subsequent police investigation there was a large media focus on the weapon and how it had been obtained. It is certainly fair to have concerns over the availability of firearms; a man with intent to mass murder can do far less damage with a knife compared to a gun. However, in our circumstances, the presence of the gun and its history were incidental. We would have liked to have known its origin rather than not. However, a man intent on murdering his family has many means by which to do so. The vast majority of domestic homicides involve no firearms.[3]

The fierce condemnation of the gun struck us because of its sharp contrast to the innumerable apologists for our father. How could there be such active condemnation of the passive gun but not the man who pulled the trigger several times? The issue was not that condemnation was lacking, but that the lens of blame was focused on our mother and sister and the inanimate weapon, not the one agent whose choices created the event.

Society frequently and preferentially blames weapons for murders, short skirts for rape or alcohol for assault. There are many people who can hold a shotgun, yet pose no danger to anyone. Likewise, many men, on encountering an inebriated woman, lost and alone in the early hours of the morning, would offer guidance to ensure her safe return home. It is possible to drink alcohol and yet maintain control of one's actions and act respectfully and compassionately to others. These are merely excuses.

Throughout, there was no mention of the true danger to society: the fact that an 'ordinary' man can hold such broken beliefs that he feels justified in killing his family after inflicting decades of emotional, psychological and financial abuse on them. There was little concern to find out where those beliefs had come from, despite an intense will to find the gun's source. We should not be concerned with what was being held in our father's hands, but instead what was being held in his mind.

We experienced many people quoting verbatim the same myths and the same broken stereotypes. These parroted phrases were ripped straight from the reporting and we felt trapped in an echo chamber. We knew the endings to each sentence after just a few words. Behind these opinions and myths were weakly veiled attempts to justify and rationalise what had happened. It was clear that there was guilt towards what had happened to our family, but it was also clear that there was the desire to throw this guilt off, to change nothing and continue with life as usual.

A distinctly disturbing pattern was that these myths were propounded not only in the press or by men, but even by close female friends of our mother. Some asked if our mother had had an affair, somehow believing that the events entertained the question and apparently believing that if she had, which she hadn't, it would somehow 'explain' what had happened. Others described how difficult divorce can be and how deeply he must have been suffering, apparently suggesting that divorce is somehow worse than murder. There were questions about whether the murders were 'because' of money, 'because' our father resented his children, and about why our mother had stayed for so long.

This line of questioning was intent on finding the 'because'. The presupposition was that our father was justified and all that was required was an exploration of the possible reasons until they inevitably found the 'correct' one. This would lead to a soothing reassurance that our belief systems were correct all along and that we could all go back to how things were.

This was a powerfully corrupt use of reason. Throughout the rationalisations, our sister, Charlotte, was entirely ignored. Each attempt to find a justification held dogmatically to the view that this was somehow to be expected in a marriage.

The trivialities scraped together were not 'reasons' to kill your family. Yet, there remained a persistent belief that a man is entitled to kill his family when they do not obey his arbitrary, shifting and hypocritical rules. If someone wants to kill they will find a 'reason'. Only a small mind has the rigidity and boundedness to provide such apparent certainty. Any 'reason' propounded by evil has no validity. It is obscene to believe that it does or to search on our father's behalf. Those who choose to be good will always find reasons to be good and those who choose evil will always find reasons to be evil.

We have long since grown weary of victim-blaming and murderer-sympathising. The childish simplicity of these questions is a form of oppressive ignorance that needs to be challenged. We have a role not just to avoid propagating corrupting values and distorting myths, but to actively dismantle them.

The reality of domestic abuse is highly complicated and unique in every situation. The truth for many is that we can't stay, and we can't leave. We have no options as these have been shut down systematically by the abuser. When self-sealing rationalisations also serve to trap us, our situation becomes very isolated indeed.

The true test of our tolerance was exceeded when one journalist called the killing of our mother and sister 'understandable'. The same journalist then argued that a man killing his children and wife 'is often a twisted act of love'. This was not just a regurgitated and outdated myth, but evil rationalised. This commentary removed the veil before our eyes; behind it we finally saw the pervasive sexism that saturates male and female minds alike in the realm of domestic abuse. It demonstrated the structural inequalities in how we perceive acceptable behaviour for men and women differently. It could be interpreted that some did not dare to confront the reality that this was a duplicitous individual capable of unimaginable cruelty. However, even for the sake of 'balance', we shouldn't be voicing psychopaths into the argument.

It appeared that after significant 'balancing', the argument had settled on stripping responsibility away from the actions of a killer and sympathising with his position. Throughout, there was a refusal to recognise that this was the culmination of a history of domestic abuse. In fact, the words 'domestic abuse' were rarely mentioned in the reporting. In most cases they were omitted entirely.

The commentary that we witnessed demonstrated that domestic abuse is not only condoned, it is apparently widely endorsed. It is possible to simply express sorrow about an event. It is entirely different to question victims and to praise the character of a murderer. This is not only disrespectful, but it reinforces in existing abusers' minds that what they're doing is OK and helps to sustain those belief systems responsible for the murder of women and children by men.

Men who kill their families don't perceive that they have done something evil: they believe that they are entitled to destroy their family when it no longer submits to them. A man killing the women closest to him isn't a random, unpreventable event and it doesn't happen in a vacuum. It occurs because the conditions in which these beliefs may grow are readily defended by those around him.

Our father murdered because he felt entitled to control and own his family, to cause us pain and suffering, and to take away our lives whenever our existence no longer served him. Our father had no breakdown and no collapse of his belief system. He simply followed the views that he had always held to their conclusion with no concern for us as human beings. Our father considered us as no more than his possessions.

Society often assumes that our minds can endure sensationalist headlines while maintaining a clear perception of values and the world. The dominant belief is that sensationalist headlines just provide a little excitement to our days. It's clear to us both that this is not true.

Currently, victims of domestic abuse are lumbered with the burden of having to run away as though they were fugitives. They must also endure the disapproving glare of society while they remain incarcerated in refuges for their own safety. Meanwhile, abusers and murderers are eulogised in the press and by those who 'knew' them. After the victims are hunted down and killed, they are posthumously examined and questioned. Somehow, with no one to speak for them, they are supposed to justify everything that happened to them within a system of logic where they can never be right.

Flashback – Shadow of Her Former Self

'It's a shame we can't go for coffee out any more, Claire, I used to enjoy our little cakes and treats.' Mum's friend settles into the chair in the kitchen and strokes the dogs. 'Although your dogs are lovely!'

'I know,' Mum sighs. 'He won't let me have the money to go out.'

'I can buy the next one, Claire, don't you worry.'

'He won't let me do that either.' Mum looks embarrassed.

'What? He won't let you go for a coffee even if someone else pays?'

'It's the fuel; he records the odometer. He says we don't have enough money for fuel.'

'WHAT? He won't let you work more hours and even told you not to go for that promotion! Then he says you don't have enough money for fuel?! I'll pick you up and we'll go for coffee, Claire.'

'I would love to,' Mum pauses, 'but he wouldn't like that either. I know it sounds silly, it's totally ridiculous. But he kept me up all night accusing me of having an affair with you.'

'WHAT?! Claire, we're two women. We're both married. What on earth is he on about?'

Our father disconcertingly opens the door to the kitchen and walks in without acknowledging our mother or her friend. He moves to the corner of the room, pulls out a chair and sits down.

Mum and her friend glance over to see what he is doing and notice he is just sitting, looking out of the window in silence.

After a pause, Mum breaks the silence. 'Charlotte's got all her offers for university back now, I'm so proud of her. She's worked really hard.'

'She deserves it, she's a very intelligent and lovely young lady.'

After attempting to sustain the conversation for a few minutes, and with our father still lingering, Mum suggests, 'Let's go and chat with Charlotte in the living room!'

Mum and her friend both rise from the table and move to the living room. As they sit down and begin chatting with Charlotte, our father enters too. Once again, he sits in the corner and stares silently out of the window.

Everyone is tense, knowing their conversation is being monitored.

After a while of awkward conversation, Charlotte starts playing with the dogs. She opens the door and goes outside with them. Mum and her friend follow. After a minute, our father comes outside, pulls up a deckchair and sits in their view.

'Mum, this is scary,' Charlotte whispers.

'Don't worry, darling, it's just your father, he does things like this sometimes.' Mum attempts to calm Charlotte's concerns, but she is clearly angry and also very embarrassed.

'I'd better leave to get the dinner on now. It was lovely seeing you both,' Mum's friend says, waving goodbye to Mum and Charlotte.

'That's the last time I have anyone over. I feel physically sick,' Mum utters under her breath, as she waves goodbye.

Catch a Cold and Die of Cancer

Despite the convenience of believing that what our father did was unpredictable, random, unstoppable, 'incredibly rare', 'understandable' or justified in some way, the truth is that we can prevent such events, but it requires deep introspection individually and collectively to solve. There are readily identifiable patterns of male violence against women and children. In fact, these are often carried out by what society considers 'ordinary men' with 'traditional masculine views' that, as we saw, society is willing to stand by in times of crisis. If we continue to hold these belief systems, men will continue to murder women and children, and we will continue to be surprised. We struggle to understand the things we make no effort to understand. The issues of domestic abuse and gender violence are woven into our collective belief structures.

On occasions where we are confronted with the problems concerning our definition of masculinity, we often obfuscate the issue to prevent us having to dive into its murky waters. A common approach is to attempt to hide a killer in the nebulous realm of mental illness.

However, this misrepresents mental illness. There is a difference between a cold and cancer. There is also a difference in the mental realm between sadness and a desire to murder. Even more so, there is a key difference between a mental instability that is self-inflicted through choice and one that is beyond an individual's control. When we look to understand 'depression' in an abuser, we find its roots lie in frustrated attempts to subordinate those whom they wish to control. An abuser may become 'depressed' if they feel their arbitrary entitlement being challenged. However, it cannot be said that this 'depression' is in any way legitimate as it is the result of their own oppressive disregard for the mental state of others. If abusers choose to treat other humans like objects, they are bound to be disappointed when humans protest and continue to demand basic human rights. It is therefore lazy to lump wildly differing conditions into the catch-all category of 'mental illness'. Not all 'mental illnesses' deserve our sympathy.

This societal pity for 'sad' men creates the 'instinctive man' domestic abuse archetype. This instinctive man has no options but to carry out his urges and instincts. Society perceives nothing wrong with this idea of man as a regressive infant. In fact, it seems to generate a collective urge to comfort and cuddle him like a small child. This is the reality of regressed masculinity.

The woman harmed in any act by the instinctive male is condemned for every eventuality and possibility that she did or didn't take. Women are burdened with infinite responsibility for every hypothetical scenario we can imagine. While the instinctive man is relieved of responsibility for the choices he does make, the woman is considered responsible for reducing the man to this regressive state.

Following such rationalisations of male mental illness, sympathy is heaped on male killers for how they were let down. It is lamented how no one asked how they felt, gave them a hug or some other responsibility-denying excuse. How we let women down is apparently their problem. We grant men power in the household and then bemoan that they did not have the support they needed. If our father wanted an open environment, he had all the power he needed to create one. He cannot have it both ways.

Explaining our father's actions as if they were a result of

others' behaviour or events denies that he had autonomy. These explanations implicitly sought to demonstrate that there was underlying logic to his actions or that he was not responsible for controlling his emotions through choice like the rest of us. This was particularly difficult for us to swallow when women are examined under a microscope for their 'choices' in instances of domestic abuse. This attitude reinforced our father's responsibility-denying logic that we were to blame for everything that happened to him. It pretended that he was right; that there was a 'reason' in the external world that 'caused' him to behave in a certain way. If we don't believe in our own free will, then our lives are entirely pointless as we have no ability to shape them. Determinism is not a guide to living, it is an excuse not to live.

Explaining the story from our father's perspective looked to understand a killer rather than to seek to understand the innocent victims of despicable violence. Forgiveness is not a fitting response to what happened to us, on a societal or individual level. Forgiveness is a form of amnesia and numbness; an apathy. It removes us from the context of our lives and disconnects us from the actions that our lives demand.

Despite these flaky rationalisations, it was evidently clear that our father didn't 'lose it'. He was functioning as he always had, and that's the problem. There are many ordinary men just like him with the capacity for violence. It does not derive from mental illness; it derives from responsibility-denying entitlement. Our father was always the man that the world saw on 19 July 2016. He did not suddenly change. That was the one thing he always refused to do.

An oppressor uses his power to derive value and esteem from how effectively he subjugates his subordinates. Our father brutalised us growing up. It is contradictory to feel sympathy for someone who used their power in such a way. We were struck that it seemed easier for many to sympathise with killers than victims. There appeared to be some mystical and unfounded idea that if someone is punished or suffers misfortune then they must have deserved it. A belief in the idea that the world is fair carries with it the idea that we deserve everything that happens to us; that bad things happen for a 'reason'. This fundamentally leads us to turn on victims with the implicit demand that they must have somehow done something to 'deserve it'. The consequence of this victim-blaming was that a call to action to tackle domestic abuse was entirely missed.

As men who have suffered under this broken ideology of masculinity, we believe that all men must learn to stand on their own two feet, not supported by the creaky and unstable rationalisations of a society which will endlessly forgive men for their flaws. We need men who can sustain themselves and others.

In 2018, in the UK and Republic of Ireland, almost 4,700 men took their own lives, a figure three times that of women.[4] Men are less inclined to communicate feelings of despair or hopelessness and are more likely to present a stoic attitude towards misfortune.[5] Men also tend not to seek help for emotional difficulties, often feeling that help-seeking is a weakness or failure.[6] The cause of this suffering is not something external to men. It is men suffering from exactly the same masculinity that women and children are persecuted by. It is masculinity turned against itself. These traditional masculine beliefs prevent men from acknowledging their situation and accepting help. It is clear from these male suicide statistics that we all need to be saved from these broken masculine ideals.

Power over others is not strength; it is weakness projected into the world. True strength comes from command over ourselves. We need to teach men the true language and behaviours of strong men, not the contradictory rationalisations of weak and resentful murderers. Masculinity as it currently stands is a zero-sum game on a single power spectrum. Some men, like our father, interpret the rules of this game to mean that competitive destruction is required to 'succeed' against others. When these men feel that they can no longer compete within the rules that masculinity has defined for them, they believe they have nowhere to go. The only solution these men believe that they have is their own destruction and the destruction of the world. However, there is always somewhere to go; these men have mistaken their belief systems for the limits of the world.

It is strange to see these self-emasculated men, like our father, struggle against the masculinity that oppresses them while explicitly campaigning for it. These misogynous men vehemently attack women and feminism, yet their weakness is internal. Men must learn to define themselves within themselves, not always pursuing a weaker other on which to build their identity. It seems that masculinity is often defined by what it is not rather than what it is.

Unable to stand on its own two legs, it must be propped up by its subordinates. Unless we actively address the role of men in society, this crisis of masculinity will result in more deaths.

While we continue with our current beliefs we will continue to give sympathy to men because of their 'emotional reactions'. Are men that weak and 'sad' that they are entitled to kill to relieve their sadness? Shouldn't we condemn these individuals rather than give them sympathy? Our emotional reactions are determined by the values that we have cultivated. Our actions are motivated by those very same values. We are responsible for our character which is the source of these values.

We need to be careful how we respond to such men. The way we currently respond is not even in men's interests. We are creating weak men who feel immense self-pity and are unable to endure life's challenges because they expect women to do so much for them. If we accept that men's understandable response to an ordinary life event is to murder, then we should seriously consider a society without men. If men were condemned to violence and hatred then this would be the only sensible solution, but we know that isn't true because that's not what lives inside of us. Currently society encourages weakness in men; unstable men then enter an all-or-nothing mentality as they believe vulnerability is not an option at any cost. In this decision they have cut off the only possible way to confront their flaws and overcome them. They would rather die and kill than change. Someone who is willing to kill others and themselves is not someone who is happy or at peace.

Therefore, we must not propound such unreasonable and irrelevant expectations for human beings as we currently do with gender roles. We often laugh at the fundamentalism of previous ages and how their broken beliefs caused them to act in the most ridiculous ways. Our story demonstrates that broken ideologies are alive and well.

Murders like those committed by our father are entitled suicides. They combine the cowardice of the fear of dying alone with the narcissism of believing they have the right to take others with them. The issue is not men, but masculinity. Men must bring to the world what the world needs. We do not need cheap tyrants who demand that the world conform to their selfish wishes and who will bring the world down to stand higher upon its ashes. We need strong men and women to stand side by side. There are plenty of problems we must solve that we are all needed for.

Flashback – Table for One

LUKE

Ryan, Charlotte and I are all sat on the chairs in the living room stroking the dogs and doing our homework on a Saturday morning. The sun is streaming through the windows and it's a beautiful day. Mum comes in from the kitchen.

'Luke, Ryan, Charlotte, can you all follow me to the kitchen please?'

I get up first. Ryan and Charlotte are right behind me. It's 2006, I'm revising for my upcoming GCSE exams and I'm frustrated that I have to stop working. It's almost certainly another pointless thing our father wants to reprimand us for. Once again, he's forced our mother to collect us to make it look like she's the one enforcing all the rules.

We all take our seats; our father is already sitting down at the head of the table. He looks ready to scold us, as usual.

'I've got something to tell you,' Mum tentatively announces.

Our ears prick up. This isn't normally how these meetings go. I'm concerned by Mum's tone. She has her usual stoic face on and it's hard to see that anything is up from her expression, but the slightest hint of fear in her voice is enough to focus our attention.

Mum doesn't look at any of us, and without skirting around the subject begins talking, staring down at the table in front of her.

'I've got cancer.'

I listen a little bit longer, but there is nothing. My mind takes time to process what it has heard as it stutters trying to understand the consequences.

'What does that mean, Mum? Are you going to be OK?' Charlotte asks with a lone tear sliding down her cheek.

Ryan and Charlotte both begin gently sobbing. I'm still trying to process what I've just heard.

'Well, I . . .' Mum begins.

'Do you idiots know what it's like having a wife who's got cancer?! This is stressful for me too. And the stress you lot cause is why I got my prostate cancer,' our father snaps at all of us. 'You don't care when I'm ill. You didn't care when I had cancer.'

Our father is playing the victim yet again. Initially, I'm shocked but very quickly I become incredibly angry. I see his childish, entitled face spewing rage at us. I'm no longer listening to the words; all I see is a pitiful, pathetic old man who has never grown up and cannot handle it when the attention is not focused on him.

I could get up and crush him right now.

Our mother bursts into tears at our father's behaviour and Ryan and Charlotte begin sobbing even more intently.

After a while of this, and with no sign of him backing down from his selfish rant, I feel the anger building within. Everything turns red with rage and I can barely see my father through the fire that has engulfed me. I'm no longer thinking, my awareness is now in my muscles, in my strength and in my determination. I feel as if I'm growing into a giant but I feel so light, as if I'm almost rising off the floor. The past and the future disappear. All that matters is my desire to destroy my father.

I take a deep breath and swallow the burning fire inside me. A fight would only make this situation worse.

'You're an idiot! Everything always has to be about you. When will you grow up?' I stand up and confront him.

He wanted this and begins escalating as usual. 'This isn't your house, Boy! You live here under my rules or you can fuck off. In fact, all of you can fuck off!'

'Why do you always make everything so shit?!' I snap.

He grabs me by the shirt and drags me outside. I no longer see him as a human being; I'm certain he's not. He's a heartless coward and we'd all be better off without him.

In fact, our life would have always been better without him.

'Pack your stuff, Boy!'

'You're making it worse for Mum!' I insist.

'I'll look after the woman! You're old enough to look after yourself, now fuck off!'

Through the window into the kitchen, I see Mum, Ryan and Charlotte all hugging. I can see them looking at me, through their tears, concerned about what might happen next.

I take another deep breath. I'm not going to hit him, that will just make all of this worse for everyone. I look him in the face.

'I'm not going anywhere while you're still around.'

Wrapped up Warm in Contradictions

In those days and weeks following the murders we had to endure the eulogising of our father. We once again had to see the world from his perspective. As if he had never gone, we had to endure the same constant questioning of our mother and sister that we had suffered growing up. It seemed that many of the loudest voices were simply our father's voice thrust back at us again.

The few voices that spoke up against the prevailing apologist interpretations of our father's behaviour were generally ignored. Once the reinforcement of our father was complete, the coverage finished. It never resolved anything.

Locals and newspapers had simply attempted and failed to explain how a 'good man' could kill his family rather than acknowledging that this was a terrorist who had lived in clear sight. Many simply believed that if they could explain his actions, then they had resolved the issue. After a handful of 'reasons' had been dug out of dusty drawers, it was concluded that one of these must be right or, on aggregate, they explained enough to move on.

Existing myths about domestic abuse were successfully propagated and reinforced once again. Unfortunately, the disparate nature of domestic abuse means we never appreciate its full consequences.

We were overcome with the vast swamp of contradictions and denial that we encountered following the murders. Given the silent suffering of victims of domestic abuse, victim-blaming and sympathising with the murderer do not help. Silence of victims leads to yet more violence. We must encourage victims to speak and persevere to hear their stories.

We were shocked by the chronic failure to appreciate that there may have been a backstory for us, our mother and our sister. However, there were plenty of fabricated backstories for why our father was justified to kill. We so rarely hear about victims that they occupy so very little of our consciousness.

One particularly defunct excuse provided on our father's behalf was that 'he must have had a difficult childhood'. There was not even the question of whether he did. We were presented with the assertion, in his favour, that it was hard; hard enough to kill in fact. This was apparently not up for discussion. We just didn't understand how diffi-culty can push people to a murderous place.

This response to our tragedy dumbfounded us. Innu-merable contradictions and inconsistencies collided in our minds. There was so much we could say against this that our mouths clogged and we remained speechless, unable to utter a single response.

As far as we're aware our father wasn't a child soldier, he wasn't tortured by the mafia and he didn't work in the mines as an infant. The only response we needed to make was that he created a far more challenging environment for us than anything he suffered growing up. If our father's actions could be so easily excused, then our upbringing would surely entitle us to carry out supremely brutal vi-olence. Yet, this is not what we want. We do not wish to kill anyone. We wish to break the cycle of violence. Our father did not suffer extraordinary trauma growing up; he simply witnessed a patriarchal relationship between his father and mother and was infected with the belief that he was entitled to have a woman obey him when he grew up. He then created the conditions and coerced our mother to fit into her submissive position; a power relationship that he believed he was entitled to.

Talk of trauma causing abuse is a diversion. Abuse is entirely based around beliefs. Mum and Charlotte had been through so much more suffering in their lives than our father and they only chose love in response to that. They showed us that our father's behaviour was not 'understandable', it was not inevitable. Our mother and Charlotte became strengthened and more resilient in the face of insurmountable challenges. It is from their bravery and strength that we learned that evil is not an excuse and it does not irrevocably taint its victims with evil.

We often consider women as delicate and beautiful and then praise ourselves for our sensitivity. However, this can often serve to further objectify women. It is no coincidence that our father was quoted as being 'protective'. By demoting women to sensitive, fragile objects, 'protective' men rush in to operate paternalistically on their behalf and do 'what's best for them'. If women fail to understand what's in their best interests, then unfortunately they must be controlled or ultimately killed to protect them from doing something they ought not to do.

Living under our father demonstrated that we must all take responsibility for every moment of our lives. Our father relinquished responsibility at every opportunity. Everything was someone else's fault and was maliciously targeted at him. Women and men alike must take responsibility for their lives or this pattern of abuse will never stop. Women must be confident in their abilities to sustain and guide themselves. Men must build an internal source of strength and not project their weakness into the world in the form of coercive control.

Relinquishing responsibility in the world can lead to incomprehensible contradictions. Our father considered that he was a good man throughout his entire life. Self-righteous entitlement was his defining feature. On the morning of the killings, he dutifully purchased a parking ticket. He carefully prepared an obsequious note for the police on the driver's seat, providing the house keys and politely requesting that they do not break the front door down. He also excused himself for the marijuana traces that the police would inevitably find in the house and the car, lying and claiming that this was for pain relief.

The cherry on the top of this ideological authoritarian's narcissism was the paradoxical justification provided in his twelve-page murder note. He excused the murder of our mother and sister by claiming that he had always been 'non-violent'. He had learned to create a moral crown for himself which he could break whenever it suited him. He was the origin of all rules and morality; after all, it is not possible for God to be wrong; whatever God does is, by definition, good. This was his reasoning.

We cannot allow abusers to speak on behalf of victims or let victims' identities be subsumed into that of the abuser. We cannot let men define the terms of a relationship and leave behind a coerced narrative from the grave.

The commonality among those who inflict evil is a resentfulness and bitterness at the world for their own suffering. It is not logically coherent to sustain self-pity for endured pain and then thrust this pain arbitrarily into the world to create yet more suffering. Unfortunately, this cocktail of self-pity awash with entitlement and perceived victimisation is often enough to facilitate male violence like our father's.

Abusers don't consider their acts to be evil, which is why we must destroy the rationalisations behind their behaviour to prevent them from holding this stance. Otherwise, we allow them to cultivate their own psychological distortions which lead them to feel that they are provoked by the world.

We must remember that we can convince ourselves to do anything with sufficiently spurious reasoning. We are both the persuader and the persuaded; exactly as intelligent and ignorant as we need to be to develop an argument and to believe it respectively.

We must recognise that reason isn't how the world works. It is a gross simplification and our best interpretation of it. The function of reason is to take basic assumptions as far as they can go through estimations, patterns and inference, not to determine the truth in any absolute or objective sense. Certainly, reason can never be confident enough to justify murder.

Reason is simply our way of navigating one interpretation among many available to us. We must always beware of those who claim to have discovered the truth of a situation, particularly murderers. We latch onto arguments emotionally, since where we feel an argument represents us we will find any way to rationalise it. This should reveal a lot to us about our underlying belief systems. The reasoning that we observed in the media unveiled the underlying misogyny which it was attempting to justify.

The 'natural state' of human behaviour is heavily influenced by what we believe it should be. It is influenced by the behaviours we encourage and discourage in every day-to-day interaction. Each of us has a responsibility to break the cycle of violence through how we communicate. With each word, we are shaping the society around us. We need to recognise that there is never an excuse for giving in to hatred and perpetrating it against others. We must communicate the language of responsibility.

Currently, the 'common sense' view of domestic abuse is entirely the wrong way around. We condemn women's decisions and praise men for irrelevant qualities to absolve them of their responsibility.

The only way that we can understand domestic abuse is to recognise our biases and understand which perspectives we are failing to see accurately. Often when we talk about domestic abuse we implicitly assume that we are referring to women's issues. The truth is that domestic abuse is a male issue. Women suffer it, but men create it. Domestic abuse shouldn't be viewed through a lens of how well women suffer the abuse, the quality of the decisions they make and how effectively they escape it. We should be condemning the beliefs and behaviours of those men who perpetrate it and the decisions those men make.

Flashback – A Cold Heart

RYAN

It is late in the evening and there is a knock at the front door. It's a school friend, asking us out to play.

'Erm, I can't come out tonight, I have homework to do. Luke does too. Sorry,' I say, peering through the small opening in the doorway.

Without hesitation, I slam the door. I must have appeared rude, but it was necessary to prevent heat escaping from the house. My conversation cost our family money. Money that our father will have been counting for every second I was speaking.

I retreat quickly to the warmth of the living room; the only room in the house with the heating on.

'What the hell were you doing, Boy?! You had that door open for way too long. You just need to say no and shut the door. We can't afford this!' grumbles our father, momentarily looking up from his laptop.

The rest of the house is icy cold. The dogs are shut in the kitchen, with baby gates segmenting the house into zones to keep them wherever our father's whim determines.

'Can the dogs come in? It's freezing in the hall,' I ask.

'They're just dogs. Stop whining and grow up!'

'But they've been locked in the kitchen for hours.'

'If it's such a problem, we'll just get rid of them. They're only trouble!'

I realise now is a good time for me to remain quiet.

Despite the rest of us sitting in silence, our father is blasting football from the TV, while playing videos on his laptop and guffawing at the top of his voice.

'Can you please turn the TV off, Charlotte is trying to do her homework?' pleads our mother.

'Look, this is my house. I want to watch the football. I've got to deal with the boy whingeing about the dogs and you moaning about the TV. I just want to relax but you're always ganging up on me and creating problems!'

'The house is too cold for me to go anywhere else. I need to get this homework done tonight,' Charlotte pleads.

'Did you not listen, Girl? Put your headphones on! This

is my house. I work to pay the bills! Until you start paying, you can shut up!'

Charlotte reluctantly puts on her headphones to try to drown out some of the noise. It is futile to speak up.

Now that he's won, his interest in the football match has faded. Yet, he keeps the match playing on the TV with the volume turned up high. His attention returns to his laptop and he begins laughing loudly once again.

Invisible Icebergs

As we saw, the male perspective in domestic abuse is un-questioned because it is the lens that we see through. It was understood that the answers to our tragedy were not to be found in our father's choices, but to lie elsewhere. The meta-narrative seemed to be artificially shifted from 'a man murdering his wife and daughter' to 'a wife and daughter who died'. In this sleight of hand, our father's actions were excused and not even a part of the problem; a passive, unfortunate event had simply befallen our family, including our father.

There appeared to be an almost total denial of the world behind closed doors in the media interpretations. Yet, we shouldn't be surprised that cruel people, like our father, make efforts to conceal their behaviour, creating Jekyll-and-Hyde realities. People are caught off guard when they find that someone who they vaguely knew was entirely different from how they believed them to be. It should not surprise us that people can act. In fact, people act most of the time. Abusers are the most practised and effective actors. Aggressive patriarchs also behave differently around people in different contexts. They are much more likely to demand the subjugation of their dependants rather than attempting to dominate random acquaintances on the street. Society excuses people too often for private lives which cause significant harm to others.

The Jekyll-and-Hyde problem is exacerbated by the tendency towards black and white in conversations held in the public domain. There is a desire for clear distinctions. The transient and fast-paced nature of news means that there is not time to address complex moral quandaries because these make it difficult to form our beliefs and heuristics and move on to the next story. The risk is that we reinforce easily digested simplifications in lieu of true representations. Domestic abuse is only understood correctly if we accept that many of our beliefs are conflicting, contradictory and unstable. We therefore risk only seeing the side of the story that is most visible. Yet, the true nature of coercive control is hidden by abusers and easily overlooked.

Aggression, even without violence, demands subordination. It is designed to threaten and demonstrate the capability to inflict harm. It is the continual fear of violence which abusers use to cultivate their control. Actual violence is only used where it is required to inflict the fear of violence. If it is used lazily, the abuser risks becoming visible and losing control over their domain.

The problem of the strength of victims is that we often don't see those who are persevering well. When secretly arranging rental accommodation for our mother and sister, it struck us how common this process was and how expert the estate agents were at facilitating such escapes from abusive households. How much do we not know about this underworld?

Those with power in society define the language of our conversations. Language wields power through connotations which define the presuppositions of any argument and the tone of our assertions. The media therefore has a powerful moral conditioning role. However, as we experienced, the media's role as moral conditioner is often conflated with that of a sensationalist entertainment source. This contradiction risks trivialising the very messages that we should be spreading.

When the ideals of family or masculinity conflict with the reality of protecting innocent women and children, it can be tempting to pretend there is no conflict by entirely ignoring one side of the argument. However, society must solve the problems it faces, not create new ones for distraction. For example, in our case, much of the discussion following the murders was about money. Money is a convenient, anodyne perspective. It creates a tangible materialistic dimension, as far away from belief systems as we can reach.

We were concerned with the lack of moral discussion in public conversation following the murder of our mother and sister. An amoral society quickly descends into immorality due to its lack of guidance and positive conditioning. A society must not risk becoming so focused on protecting the inviolability of it beliefs that it is not willing to have a conversation about values.

Simply because many of us are not prevented from living our intended everyday lives by traditional belief structures does not imply that our society should continue in this way. Women and children's safety and freedom should prevail over any male's interpretation of ownership rights. Our beliefs should support the ways we wish to live; they should not oppress us and represent a world in which we no longer live.

Suppressing an issue does not make it go away; it festers in stagnant waters below the level of consciousness, slowly and invisibly building strength until it breaches back into consciousness stronger than before. The only way to address domestic abuse is to deal with it and its comorbid dysfunctional belief systems through honest, personal and public conversation. We cannot force women and children to resolve these issues themselves. Domestic abuse survivors have no shortage of strength. Unfortunately, the strength of enduring abusive behaviour becomes our liability as we learn to deal with unliveable situations when we should be screaming for help. Therefore, we all have a responsibility to protect women and children from abuse.

Flashback – Control at All Costs

RYAN

I come out from the exam hall having completed another GCSE exam. Everyone is energetically recollecting each answer and mistake made. I know I've done what I need to and never enjoy these moments which I find self-indulgent and a waste of time. I have the next exam to prepare for. More importantly, I know my father is here.

The clock is ticking, and I can imagine his furrowed and reddening face, his stuttering frustration and spitting anger. He will be getting more frustrated the longer I take. I walk directly to the car, with its engine running, outside the school gates.

'You're late!' my father grumbles as he accelerates aggressively down the road before I manage to engage my seatbelt.

In fact, I was exactly on time. However, given his early arrival, this has made me unforgivably late. Time operates with him as its reference, so there is no point saying anything to contradict him.

He doesn't know what exam I've taken, nor does he care. I'm grateful for the silence; I don't want to be stuck in a conversation with him anyway.

To my father, all that matters is that we get back to the house as soon as possible. You wouldn't guess that he's not working today; in fact, he has nothing planned. Even so, my GCSEs had rudely interfered with his life.

We drive in silence, the air thick with his crushing hatred as it always is around our father. Each of his deep breaths, each exaggerated gear change, each aggressive jolting brake and the look in his eyes are all warnings to me. He doesn't need words to convey his arbitrary anger – he's trained us all to respond to his subtle signals. Like Pavlov's dog, but with surges of fear and anxiety, we have learned that he controls how we feel at all times. Even when he is not around, we feel as if he is breathing down our necks.

The untrained never feel this, they only see the jovial 'protector', but these small signals are woven into his behaviour to always remind us of our place. When we are in the same room as guests who see my father as fun-loving and carefree, we are breathing different air to them and living in a different world. We are living in the world he has built inside of us, one that no one else can see or feel.

I have to be rushed home for no reason other than our father's arbitrary timekeeping, which he prides himself on. Meanwhile, my friends are out socialising and maybe playing football or sitting by the glistening river in the sun, celebrating the sensation of one less exam until freedom. I know any true freedom for me is still years, decades away even.

As we drive, between the flickers of sunlight shining through the trees, there is a flashing of headlights in our rear-view mirror. Someone wants to overtake us. Despite my father's insistence on rushing me home from my friends, he has been driving at a laboured 40mph down a 60mph country road. When our father decides things have to be done fast, he makes everyone speed up. When he decides they must be done slowly, he holds everyone up. It is everyone else's responsibility to know which side of his vacillating demands is the true side at that moment.

A van has been wanting to overtake us down this narrow country lane for quite some time. The polite request by the van driver behind infuriates my father. My father slows down further still and moves towards the middle of the road. Later, the road widens out to two lanes as we approach the village of Moulton and the van moves to overtake prior to entering the 30mph speed limit zone.

Suddenly, our father slams his foot down on the accelerator pedal.

'Dad, stop! Leave it!'

We are approaching a primary school and our car is now travelling at double the speed limit. My father winds down his window and veers to the other side of the road to pull alongside the van.

'THERE'S A PRIMARY SCHOOL THERE, YOU SHIT!' screams my father at the van driver, while our car swerves and speeds directly in front of the school gates, with parents and children walking on the adjacent paths. The van driver looks incredulously at our father, as does everyone leaving the school. He's now speeding past the van, driving the remainder of the journey through the village at 60mph. His eyes are wild. His mouth is spitting as if he were salivating after a kill.

This incident is just another implicit threat on my life. He was willing to crash because I have more to lose than him. In fact, part of him willed a fiery crash; he would have enjoyed death if it meant he could take me with him and cause as much pain as possible.

At home, I walk inside without saying a word. My father, hot on my heels, pursues me around the house, venting his incoherent self-created rage: 'You don't speak to me like that, Boy!', 'I'll teach you some fucking manners next time!', 'Stupid boy, if you talk to me like that you'll get us both killed next time!'

I sit in the corner and begin studying for my next exam

while my father continues storming around the house. Long ago, I learned to blank him out. If I am ever to live a life free of fear, I have to get my head down and work as hard as I can for a future that, at this point, I can only hope for.

I feel powerless in our situation. However, I know that success in exams is necessary in order to get the money to escape from home as soon as possible. Luke and I need to work to provide for Mum and Charlotte.

I look over at my father, sat behind his laptop. Instead of providing for his family, he repeatedly chooses to control and restrict us.

My subject choices and career options as a young boy are determined by this man's failures. How I would have loved to truly discover my interests, yet I know the arts and music will not give us the financial resources that we need.

As my father continues to yell, I feel my years spiralling past and I grieve each moment of childhood and opportunity lost. With the growing realisation of the responsibility Luke and I hold for our family's future, I begin to feel old with the burden. Yet, I know it is something that we have no choice but to pursue.

Weapons of Mass Distraction

The public look to the media to understand how they should feel about events in the world. As we witnessed, there are many who absorb these opinions and then regurgitate them in a simple pattern-matching exercise when similar events occur. If the media does not speak up en masse, then a vital opportunity to protect the vulnerable in society is lost. We never sympathise with foreign terrorists in the same way that we are willing to excuse those within our own borders. We would never dare to call a foreign terrorist's act *understandable*, to rationalise their act because of the difficulty of their childhood or the social alienation that must have driven them to such despair. Domestic abusers are ideologues in the same way as traditional terrorists. Ideologies are not moral, the world is too complicated to be governed by simple rules; ideologies are oppressive and are the tools of abusers. Where possible, oppressors often prefer to praise the 'virtues' of their victims' subordination rather than enforce repression. Abusers will often cycle between the two.

We must represent the issues of domestic abuse as they are, not how we wish them to be. Currently, the media is ready with a handful of pre-packed rationalisations to stamp on any public spillover of domestic abuse. The aim seems to be to isolate each disparate event, tie it up and box it away rather than to act to prevent patterns of abuse.

It struck us how impervious many rationalisations were to facts. For example, the common narrative was that moving out of our house was a key moment in the cascade of events. This was despite police reports noting that our father had been writing drafts of his murder note prior to us even planning to leave.

Moving out was convenient for our father because it created a pseudo-causality for the media to latch onto.

However, months before the murders he would march around the house for hours in the middle of the night. This was the same pacing that was seen before he committed suicide after killing our mother and sister. It's clear to us that he had been mentally preparing himself to kill us all for several months, potentially years.

A police report on our father's internet searches revealed that for months he had been investigating murder; one search among many read, 'How many men kill their wives?' These numerous searches indicate that our father was influenced by what he found on the internet. We do not doubt that much of the previous domestic homicide reporting that he was likely to have encountered would have reinforced his attitude.

Divorce had nothing to do with our father's actions. The murders were entirely to do with our continued subordination. He felt that he was losing his firm grip over our lives and intended to kill us for it. Yet, despite these findings, the most easily digestible version of events was our father suffering a breakdown over the four days following our escape. This readily fitted a convenient pre-packed male-sympathising narrative of how divorce can tip men over the edge: that divorce is somehow anti-male even though our mother accounted for exactly half of the divorce and also experienced it. Mum and Charlotte were never given emotional legitimacy; they were simply treated as objects in a story that focused only on our father's emotional journey. Our lives' struggles had been fitted into a Procrustean bed for the sake of the only available storytelling templates.

The greatest power abusers wield is their ability to distort reality and force the issue back into the depths of silence and ignorance. On a societal level, we hear of tragic events and intuitively think that we understand them. We rationalise that this wouldn't happen to us because we are 'good' or 'different'. This is nothing but the power of the abuser to deceive society too. Abusers disarm to facilitate their control. To assume that we know the struggles of others is to fail to learn a valuable lesson that can help us all. But delusion is sometimes the medication that provides us with a good night's sleep and a clean conscience.

It is unfortunate that often we do not believe the true severity of suffering unless we experience it or unless we are able to connect with it somehow. Therefore, education, achieved by sharing stories of suffering, is vital but we must be careful because an incorrect use of language or perspective serves to prolong broken beliefs. We cannot afford to reinforce the idea that continued suffering is OK.

These stories of suffering reinforce our collective morality. Morality is a crucial tool that allows us all to exist together beyond our individual concerns. We rely on the moral conditioning of others for our own safety. Therefore, we should all take the moral conditioning of our society very seriously.

It is clear to us that an opportunity for a societally urgent conversation on a hugely damaging and almost invisible subject was missed after our tragedy. We recognised our duty to use our voices to protect those who are vulnerable and can't afford to speak up themselves. We hope that by sharing our story we may help others to understand the reality of domestic abuse.

Unfortunately, the usual style of reporting on domestic abuse fails to teach us all the necessary lessons. The hidden truth is that domestic abuse is a form of terrorism where the masculine-fundamentalist abuser's sole purpose is to terrify, attack, trap and fundamentally kill if they are not obeyed. This is a terrorism of men against women and children. It is the result of some men choosing to interpret masculine ideals as entitlement to harm others, just as some choose to interpret religious documents in a way that justifies their claims to violence.

The smattering of disconnected and unacknowledged stories of domestic abuse in the media leave us entirely unaware of the impact of this crime. Yet, the cost of domestic violence is estimated at $8tn a year globally.[7] Domestic abuse is much more ordinary than we would like to accept. One in four women experience domestic abuse in their lives.[8] Many of us know someone who has suffered. If our streets were as violent and abuse-ridden as our homes, we would all be terrified to go outside.

Despite this brutal reality, there is no political rhetoric around domestic abuse and it is almost absent from mainstream discourse as victims remain silent from fear or are killed. There is a belief in the safety achieved by covering our eyes. Yet, while we do not address its significance, domestic abuse remains a war that women and children all over the country are abandoned to fight by themselves.

In fact, 136 UK servicemen and -women were killed

during operations in Iraq[9] and 405 during Afghanistan operations as a result of hostile actions up to the end of 2017.[10] From 2009 to 2015, in the safety of the UK, 936 women were killed by instances of male violence.[11] Globally, it is estimated that nine times more deaths are incurred as a result of violence between individuals than through war.[12] That more citizens are killed within our homes than on our battlefields must lead us to ask: where does the true danger lie? Despots within our society pose a much more lethal risk to our population and democratic values than those abroad.

These victimised women and children are not treated as heroes of our society for standing up to their oppressors when they are murdered. Instead, their lives and deaths are devalued as we sweep the reality under the rug. We close the door and we sympathise with the 'surely difficult' circumstances that drove the murderers to inflict this fate upon those they should love. In fact, even after being killed, women are often blamed for 'putting up with it' and attempting to live their lives despite their suffering. However, the very act of escaping is seen by the abuser as justification to hunt down and kill their victims: up to 75 per cent of abused women who are murdered are killed after they leave their partners.[13]

The impact of media misinformation can be lethal. We spent our lives looking for the stereotypes of domestic abuse conveyed by the media while domestic abuse continued to tear our lives apart. If the media does not shine a light on the true cause of domestic abuse then, as our story shows, we cannot expect anyone to understand the struggles and challenges that it involves, even those facing it daily.

Flashback – Where the Sun Don't Shine

RYAN

'Mum, I've got a place!' I shrieked with excitement.

I've just got back from a qualifying race for the Great Britain Age Group Triathlon team, having secured my place to race in Turkey with the national team this summer. I have been looking forward to coming home to tell Mum.

'Well done, Ryan! I knew you could do it!'

Mum is elated. Not only is she brimming with pride, but this is also going to be her first holiday in nearly a decade.

I'm full of ideas. 'We can go together! I'm so excited. I'll book the best hotel I can!'

Mum's eyes look into the near distance. With a sigh and a relieved look on her face, I can see she is already there.

My father has refused to go anywhere sunny for fear of developing skin cancer again. This was a common occurrence as he refused to hold himself accountable for his own health. He could wear sun cream, but no. That would mean admitting that he is less powerful than the sun. Power and control are everything to him. An enormous inferno of burning hydrogen and helium, 333,000 times larger in mass than the Earth. Nope, still not letting that have one over on him.

Despite this, he still frequently goes on holidays by himself, often to exactly the places he refused to let us go. But I couldn't care less what my father does or where he goes, what has bothered me ever since I was a small boy is that my mum is not let out of his sight; if he decides he's not going anywhere sunny, that means Mum can't go either.

'We'll be right next to the beach, Mum. You can have as many massages as you like and we can go out and eat dinner by the sea. It'll be really good for you!'

Mum's multiple sclerosis is slowly degrading her body; some sun and some time away from our father would help her immensely. Mum and I both know that our father is deeply concerned about how he appears in the community. He will want 'his son' to be in the local newspapers for competing in an international triathlon. There is no way he will deny me accepting this place. Plus, I'm going to need someone with me to help me arrange my equipment on race day, look after my change of clothes, and keep me inspired and motivated. He knows this. He's known this ever since it became a dream of mine three years ago.

I hear purposeful footsteps approaching, I feel my heart drop. He's heard Mum's squeal of delight and he's coming to ruin the moment, as he always does.

As my father walks in, he sees Mum and me hugging ecstatically.

'Your mum's going to stay here because she has to look after Charlotte.'

'I'm fine by myself,' Charlotte interjects.

'Stupid child, you can't look after yourself. The woman isn't going anywhere.'

Mum looks down at her feet. She knows this can't be won. We all know this can't be won.

'I'm going. I need a holiday. I have to put up with so much shit from you lot.' Our father's face is creased with a mocking smile. As quickly as he came, he turns and leaves the room.

My heart stops. Mum looks up and I look her in the eyes; I see the joy seep out of her soul. She is filled with that familiar crushing sense of helplessness.

He has done this on purpose. He has let us build up hope for these past three years, because he knew it would hurt us more when it came crashing down.

I'm stunned. 'He's spent the last ten years saying we can't go on holiday because he'll get skin cancer again. Then he does this!'

'It's OK, Ryan. I hope you have a nice time and good luck. I'm so proud of you, remember that.' Mum strains a smile, but I feel so sick and I can tell she wants to cry. I want to cry.

'I don't even want him to come. I'll go by myself!' I insist.

'You know you can't stop him, Ryan.'

Mum's right.

'But can't we go somewhere together soon – me, you and Charlotte?'

'No, because he's taken Mum's passport!' Charlotte was rummaging through Mum's documents and, as expected, Mum's passport has 'gone missing'.

He'd planned this all along. He was prepared for exactly this moment.

The Moral of the Story

Domestic abuse must be reported responsibly, and patterns of male violence must be highlighted for what they are. By the very act of choosing to talk about certain topics in the public arena and avoiding others, a society is guilty of having an agenda, even before any opinions are expressed.

Difficult conversations are the ones that we most desperately need or else we tolerate beliefs that destroy the values that ordinary people stand for. Democracy is not simply tolerating everyone's beliefs and values. That is nihilism. Democracy involves everyone having the ability to converse openly about our values and to fairly challenge them.

Currently the language used to discuss domestic abuse obscures the issue by lacking frankness. The perspectives that we take disguise the true harm and cruelty that happens while we choose not to look.

An entire world of psychological realities exists despite it not being visible to our shared perception. The beliefs and opinions that we form spill over into the world. Our father held broken beliefs about masculinity that are not uncommon. These drove his actions and his willingness to murder lay latent within these beliefs for decades. We need to place an appropriate value on the things that we cannot see. Until we do, our real world will continue to be polluted by the unaddressed issues of our psychological existence.

Unless we are honest, we will merely cover issues up until they boil over into different areas. If we tolerate victim-blaming or murder-sympathising, we are covertly demanding that victims remain silent to allow us to 'fix' societal problems that our current lack of honesty doesn't allow us to address. We simply make the problems temporarily disappear from our radar without resolving them.

The ideas that we hold onto, our traditions and our ingrained habits, are difficult adversaries. We do not need to discard entire belief systems, but we do need to re-evaluate them. While we allow broken masculine ideals to continue unchallenged, we allow social ills to propagate from the conflict they inevitably generate due to their poor fit in the world.

It's important to recognise that we need to continually change in order to grow. We need open conversations about acceptable relationship behaviours because many adults and children have no idea of the subtler signs of abuse and manipulation. In fact, if our experience is anything to go by, exposure to abuse is more likely to desensitise us further as our own virtue is turned against us by our oppressors. The prisons which confine us are often invisible because after many years we are conditioned to imprison ourselves.

Domestic abuse is also hard to prosecute. The law operates on thresholds, it doesn't function well with the aggregation of below-threshold events which characterise coercive control. The burden of evidence is enormous to prove the patterns of abuse accumulated over years, often unseen by anyone except the victim. This simply means we must work harder to protect vulnerable individuals.

Victims of abuse are taught to believe others' interpretations of events and to discard their own. Yet, our society desperately needs to hear victims' and survivors' accounts. Our society still does not work for far too many.

Initially, there will be some who react negatively to victims' and survivors' stories; the inconvenient unearthing of deeply buried truths. But, we rely on vibrant and determined minorities to change society for the better. Being outnumbered should never stop us from speaking the truth of our experience. There may be many things we cannot know for certain, but our experience is one of the very few things we can know completely. We must not be afraid to speak it.

It may feel that there is no point in speaking if there is no one to listen, but by speaking our very task is to create the listener. Currently, domestic abuse is very much something people don't wish to see or hear about. People would rather it stayed at home, behind closed doors. Those of us who have experienced its effects need to speak up so that it becomes normal for domestic abuse not to occur, not simply that we don't hear about it.

Flashback – Fraud for Board

RYAN

'Would you mind sending over the money please? Your father is having a go at me because you haven't paid yet,' pleads Mum.

'Mum, I've literally been home for one hour – it's a twelve-hour bus ride from Aberdeen, followed by two hours on the train. I need to chill out a bit first! I'm only a few weeks into my first assignment after graduating and Dad is already starting to steal my wages too.'

'I know, I know. And it's great to have you back. I love having you home, and you know that I don't want to charge you, but he insists. Your father is checking the bank account every five minutes. He won't stop until you've paid.'

I walk from the kitchen to the living room to gather my wallet.

'Where is my money, Boy?!' my father erupts from his chair in the corner of the room. 'Your mother needs this money. She can't afford to feed us if you don't pay!'

'I'm just getting my wallet.'

'Don't speak back to me or I'll bar you from this house, Boy! Just pay the money!'

I take my wallet, head back to the kitchen where Mum is preparing dinner in the cold and shut the door behind me.

As I take £100 from my wallet for the three days at home, I think what a nice earner my father has set up here.

'Mum, what does he actually do with that money?'

'I don't know, Ryan, but if he doesn't get it, he's unbearable.'

'I can't believe he claims you demand it; he must know that I'll ask you whether that's true or not.'

The door opens suddenly, and our father stands there with his arms crossed and his screwed-up face, breathing heavily.

'Work's so busy at the moment, everyone is getting ready for Christmas already, you wouldn't believe it!' Mum instantly deploys a cover conversation to perfection.

He wanted to catch us out; he wanted to catch us conspiring. Frustrated, he snatches the money out of my hand and wanders back to the living room, leaving the doors between the kitchen and living room open.

'Don't leave the bloody doors open, you're letting the heat out!' he yells, having sat back down in the living room. This is just his way of saying, 'Get in the living room where I can hear what you're saying!'

I know my mum never touches a penny of the money I send home; it's always squandered, gambled or given away to one of his internet 'friends'.

As much as I resent his dictatorship, I have to comply because he is holding my mother and sister to ransom with his enforced poverty.

4

OVERCOMING

'We acquire the strength we have overcome.'

Ralph Waldo Emerson

Sinking Feeling

From an external appearance, not only would we have seemed to be three children doing OK, we were actively succeeding in many areas of our life. At the time this appeared to be from harmless motivation and industriousness. Yet, we harboured a deep fear inside.

As children, we were blind to our strengths and weaknesses and we looked for validation of these from the external world. When the most dominant figure in our lives continually undermined every aspect of our characters, we had no image of ourselves except that which was reflected back at us; an image of failure, incompetence and guilt.

Therefore, we developed a set of social skills which were designed to keep us alert to danger and at a safe distance from others; we tried to remain hidden. We learned to communicate simply to navigate social environments with minimal conflict. We kept our heads down, only spoke when spoken to and always knew the response in case we had to answer for ourselves. We learned not to want things to avoid the disappointment of never having them. We learned to predict our father's moods and became highly perceptive of patterns and correlating factors in the run-up to him losing his temper. This process refined our intellects, yet our emotions were disregarded. Unfortunately, it isn't possible to turn down only the bad emotions, we had to shut the entire system down.

How we felt became irrelevant as we were unable to influence the circumstances of our environment. We didn't have the knowledge or the experience to be able to cope while also feeling. Our emotions seemed to only make our lives more unbearable. They felt like a failure of evolution: they appeared to have no practical purpose.

We learned to live outside of ourselves and our concerns. Our intellectualisation served to protect us from the immediate trauma by allowing us to abstract from our experiences. This enabled us to push ourselves to exhaustion for goals bigger than ourselves. The cost of this was that we were left with no idea of who we were or any idea of what we truly needed or wanted from life. However, pinning our hopes on the world around us meant that we often 'succeeded' in the eyes of others.

This escapism served as a short-term palliative; however, in the longer term, as we've learned, any escapist urge which we had not relinquished led to perpetual anxiety. Our minds learned to look for a way out of every situation and planned for every eventuality. In this state, our minds found every reason to fear life.

We never realised our situation was worse than anyone else's because there was no expectation gap. This is what we expected from life. We expected life to be unpleasant, but we worked hard to find happiness where we could and to succeed despite the demands we faced. We not only met each of these challenges, but we continued to excel because we'd grown up in an environment where success wasn't just an option, but the absolute bare minimum we could get away with. We had to succeed if we had any chance of escaping our father and looking after our mother and sister in the future.

Even though we did everything we could to oppose our father's toxic influence, in many areas of our life we were conditioned to perceive that we were the problem. Despite the stress of our home environment, our father would not permit expressions of our emotions. What we weren't allowed to express remained locked inside and this generated powerful emotional storms.

Our father often enjoyed unsettling us and generating confusion; in particular, he gaslighted daily in mundane, everyday circumstances. He would purposely relocate his own possessions around the house so that he could angrily accuse us of misplacing them. Gaslighting has such a powerful effect because it teaches you not to trust the messages from your own body: lack of confidence isn't *not believing in ourselves* so much as *not believing ourselves*. Fundamentally, our lives taught us not to believe the instructions of our minds or impulses. In the end it didn't matter what we thought, our father demanded ownership of our perception.

Despite this loss of emotional balance in the world, when we were asked how we were, we had learned to answer with a disinterested 'fine' so as not to draw attention to ourselves. Attention was almost always bad and precipitated aggression from our father; we learned to divert it or at least keep it to a minimum.

Despite playing with our minds as if they were mere playthings, our father did not like to be confronted with his cruelty. He wanted control but was angered when he had to encounter reactions from us which illuminated his hypocritical self-righteousness. Therefore, we learned to detach our external appearance from our internal realities to minimise his anger. Eventually, we learned to detach from our internal state itself.

As Spinoza said: 'Emotion, which is suffering, ceases to be suffering as soon as we form a clear and precise picture of it'.[1] However, when we tried to interpret our emotional reality we were only able to unpack our experiences through the ideas and the words that we had available. We didn't have the right concepts so our emotions fell into the abyss of unaddressed psychological trauma which we began to lose track of.

Our inability to understand what was happening to us crippled us. This led to feelings of humiliation and shame. Much of what drove that despair was feeling separate from our idea of humanity; pain evolved from our inability to comprehend our difference to our ideas of who we should have been. Talking helps us to understand each other and generate a sense that we are part of the human family. However, back then, isolated and silenced by our father, it didn't take long until we fell into such despair.

As we lost connection to the deeper parts of ourselves, we began to guide our lives by abstract moral principles rather than by the everyday emotions of ordinary adolescents. We knew we had to develop our characters for a different future, but, in the meantime, we had to become immune to the emotional and intrapersonal disruption generated by our father.

Our father's emotional and psychological attacks increased in fervour when he sensed weakness and perceived that he was making progress in grinding us down. Therefore, we learned to detach from ordinary social mirroring and reciprocation to isolate ourselves from the toxic effects of his onslaughts. Eventually he would become bored and stop when he felt it was having no effect. However, despite our appearances, our father's arbitrary and unpredictable outbursts led us to fear events like birthdays and Christmas which would draw attention to us.

No one saw that anything was wrong because all our scars and wounds were on the inside. Some regarded us as 'weird' but this was attributed to our distorted academic achievements and nerdy stereotypes.

Our detachment dehumanised us and stole the sensations of life. Our bodies wouldn't use our broken souls in the way that they would avoid using broken bones; we were protected from the continual trauma of living under our father by an existential coma. Our minds recognised that we needed a new system of living and left us in a perceptual purgatory.

As deep disorientation dug its teeth in, we tried to support our psychological weight on our fragile understanding of the world. However, each time the floor of our beliefs collapsed beneath us. Eventually, we smashed through everything we believed in with an intellectual sledgehammer to see what could withstand the battering. We continued to fall until we ended up in a barren pit of scepticism; when we had no control and nothing made sense, we chose to believe in nothing.

In this place, it felt as though we were only distant observers of the world. We saw everything unfolding yet were too far away to be involved. We were the unobserved observers. We saw things without values, as they were beyond human intention. Our adolescent trauma was like watching the world unfold inside a TV without sound, where everything seemed ridiculous and without context. The scrunching of faces and impassioned body language that we witnessed in daily life all seemed to be for nothing. Everything seemed to be for nothing.

We were not only detached from the world but also from ourselves. All basic human instincts were thrown off. We had to operate every function of our body like a puppeteer or else it would have fallen into stasis.

This was the effect of prolonged trauma during youth. The only coping mechanism we had was a disconnectedness to protect the most fundamental parts of ourselves from the gangrenous spread of psychological abuse.

The damage done to children living under domestic

abuse is extensive. Children who grow up under domestic abuse have no normal to recalibrate their experiences to after they escape abuse. Their normal is distorted and their normal becomes abuse. This distortion is then wired into their developing brains.

We have had to learn how to live again, from scratch. As children, we had to self-amputate entire parts of our emotional and psychological lives in order to literally save our lives. As adults, we have had to tear away entire parts of ourselves that were tangled inside us. We have had to give up entire possibilities in our lives because of what the abuse took away.

Most importantly, we have lost our mum and Charlotte and the lives we would have lived together.

Flashback – Constant Inconsistency

RYAN

The sound of the gravel rolling under the car's tyres always alerts the dogs to our arrival home. Mum, Charlotte and I have been out for our Saturday afternoon swim together. Today, however, something is different. We can't see the three faces of our dogs pressed up against the living room's window. The absence of the normally familiar barking creates an eerie silence. I immediately notice our father's car has gone and some windows are still open.

I rush to the house with the keys, but notice the door is already ajar. I push it open and call out the dogs' names.

Mum, Charlotte and I split up to search the house, desperately heading upstairs and downstairs; nothing.

'He's taken the dogs!' I stutter, fearful of what he will do to them.

'He's left the entire house open, what was he thinking?' Mum replies.

This is one of his favourite tricks. He will suddenly and irresponsibly disappear. Sometimes he disappears by himself with no warning, sometimes taking the dogs, sometimes taking money, sometimes going on holiday. If anything happens as a result of his actions it will be our fault. We always have to clear up after him to ensure nothing untoward happens.

I pick up his laptop and open up the Google history. Our father lives on the internet; every thought and idea of his is processed through a Google or forum search.

'He's taken the dogs to the marsh.'

He left in this manner to make a statement. We know when he returns we will have to deal with another of his angry rants. We can picture his infuriated face and mumblings as he stumbles around the marsh rehearsing every word of the rambling condemnation he is planning to deliver on his return. He will have let the dogs off their leads with no concern for their safety. We can only hope that they'll come home safe.

We hear his car pull onto the drive. We feel the winds of an incoming storm. The present silence fills our minds with tension, a fear of the contrast we are about to witness.

The door flies open. His grizzly face is streaming complaints before he's even entered.

'Fill the car up, Woman!' our father yells as he comes through the door. 'You've let it run out of petrol again. And where's my bloody dinner? I've been out all day, what the hell have you been doing? Do something useful with yourself for fuck's sake! Don't just stand there!'

As we all stumble to battle stations to help get dinner ready, our father stands in the kitchen, yelling out detailed commands: 'Clean that plate properly, Woman, I'm not eating off that!', 'Are you stupid, Girl? That's not where the sieve is stored', 'Get out of my way, dog!', as he paces up and down the room, and the dogs scuttle under the table in fear.

Each moment drags on with our father's glare burning into our backs, but at last the food is ready. Our father sits at the head of the table, eating with a scowl on his face. We all eat in delicate silence except for our father spitting frustrations: 'Stop playing with your food, Girl!' Charlotte can never eat around our father.

If there is any conversation between the rest of us, our father shuts it down, calls us idiots and demands silence.

Now he's finished, he starts giving Charlotte's food to the dogs, without even addressing her.

'Dad, don't! You'll kill them!' Charlotte screams in tears.

'Don't be a fucking idiot, child! It's only food.'

'They can't eat onions, Dad!'

'Well, they'll bloody learn what they can and can't eat, won't they!'

'They'll learn.' This is his favourite phrase. This accompanies every one of his unreasonable behaviours. It is true, we will all learn. We will all learn how little space we have for action and how he destroys aspects of our lives with his authoritarian enforcement of his trivial rules.

Maybe one day, we'll learn how much better life could be away from him. Maybe one day, it'll be a reality.

Optical Illusions

Our stereotypes and beliefs of domestic abuse shaped how we interpreted our situation growing up. They meant that we discounted the reality of the domestic abuse that we were suffering. We dismissed our experiences as ordinary growing-up experiences because of those beliefs. We had to account for the discomfort of our lives in another way: blaming ourselves. This system of thinking was shaped by our father's actions towards us; the aggregation of decades of conditioning telling us that this was ordinary. It wasn't until the murder of our mother and sister that we began to unravel his system of lies.

Those false beliefs distorted our understanding of the world that we lived in. We only saw our lives unfold through the interpretations that we believed explained them. Unfortunately, our father held the privileged position of defining the solitary narrative of our existence. Those false beliefs were the world that we lived in.

We had unfortunately applied more truth to our stereotypes of domestic abuse than to the very real emotional reality within us which told us that we were not safe. We were convinced to understand our senses of unease, anxiety and stress as our own failings by a belief system that only interpreted them as weaknesses. It seems a strange order of precedence, but it's unlikely that we are alone in this.

Once our father's narratives had persisted for long enough they were subsumed into our subconscious. We then became enslaved by their invisible sway over us.

Our father held broken beliefs on the ideals of masculinity, fatherhood and being a husband. As he took these ideals to their extreme, he was forced into a denial of his humanity; the ultimate contradiction. He failed to understand that the true test of a belief is not whether we will kill or die for it, but whether we can live it.

The world that we have experienced is only a small part of the entire world and we cannot become jaded because of the isolated segment we have endured. We cannot assume we understand the things we have not seen.

In building ourselves back up, we are learning not to allow our past to weigh us down. In general, for all of us our past experiences are supposed to be our model of existence and to guide us into the future. We have the responsibility to cultivate our mind to be the truest representation of the world. If our past is distorted by confrontations with evil, then we must recognise that our past is no longer an accurate model for the future and discard it.

We have learned that we must always choose the present over the past. Our perspective is simply our rationalisations woven to connect the dots of our experiences. These rationalisations are no truer than the many other available possibilities. If we think we have been subjected to injustice, this is only one lens. In some way we will have been lucky; there are many ways that we could have suffered further injustice.

Each new moment gives our past a new context and a new trajectory. Our lives are forever in the act of becoming and we always have the choice of who we will be in the next moment. The past injustice that we have suffered does not define us, our overcoming it does. We refuse to let who we are stop us from becoming who we want to be.

There are always going to be things that we wish had not happened or future possibilities which are no longer available to us. In fact, if we wished to play this game we would find infinite such instances. This will only lead us to resentment and bitterness.

A key lesson we have learned in the battles with our father is that our emotions are struggles we must learn to overcome ourselves. The links that naturally formed between what we felt and the external world were often oversimplified or wrong. It is strange how frequently we blamed the world for what existed within us. We have no control over the world, but we have total control over ourselves. Our healing lies within us.

Fundamentally, there are as many worlds as there are living beings. The world that we live in is one we have created for ourselves inside of us. The world in front of our eyes is therefore shaped by the world behind them. Our beliefs form the structures and systems that our lives operate by. We, and only we, have responsibility for what exists inside us. We create a new world each time we change our beliefs.

From our suffering we have learned that our feelings

are not the goal of our lives, although they do convey important messages. We have learned that often it doesn't matter how we feel when we have a greater purpose. Pain becomes destructive when we are plagued with nihilism and don't live a life we consider meaningful. Yet, we often look forward to and enjoy pain where we perceive it as the strengthening of our capacity and the reminder of our cause.

In any case, if we are too concerned with our feelings we will become fragile and weak, as our father did. If our emotional state becomes our goal in life, then negative experiences will destroy us because we will believe that nothing exists beyond how we feel.

Flashback – Pack Your Bags

'Ignore him, Charlotte. I'm proud of you and you've made the right decision. I'll always love you. You need to do what makes you happy.'

Charlotte is sobbing. Her body is wrenching from the pain, her shoulders rising and falling with each sob.

Our father remains seated in the car with his arms crossed, his red face muttering complaints.

Mum opens the car's boot and inserts the bags she's carried from Charlotte's university bedroom. They are heavy and it was a long walk. She welcomes putting them down.

Our father turns his head to berate them both. 'Bloody waste of money! Student loans for nothing! You either go to university or you don't. You've made your decision now! That's it, you can go and find yourself a bloody job the second you get back! You're not staying with us any more! You better learn how to look after yourself quick, Girl!'

Charlotte resumes her sobbing even more intently.

'Pathetic!' our father spits, and turns to look away again.

Mum hugs Charlotte. 'You can either help or shut up!' Mum responds angrily.

Our father just laughs at the rebuttal and resumes muttering to himself.

'Come on, Charlotte, I'll get the rest of the bags, come with me.' Mum puts her arm around Charlotte and they both go back to Charlotte's room to collect the last batch of her belongings.

'Charlotte, you can do whatever you want. Of course, you can stay at home, but I think for your sake it would be best if you didn't. Not with your father around. I'd love to have you with me, but I think you'd be happier if you stayed with friends.'

Charlotte reaches in to give Mum a large hug and sobs into her chest.

'And you can do whatever you want with your future. I know how much this decision has been caused by your father's behaviour. You need to stop worrying about me, you don't need to look after me. You need to plan your future and let me sort mine out.

'I'll help you plan next year for your teaching degree. Nursing isn't for you, and that's fine. There's nothing wrong with that, you didn't know until you started. Now you can plan ahead. You've got eight months until the next year starts. Take some time out and I'll make sure you get looked after.'

Why Be Good?

It is the perverse nature of the human mind that we are never content with what we have. We do not value things easy to come by and will always want things we do not have. Strangely, however, this perpetual striving means that trauma and suffering bring with them the deepest rewards if they can be overcome. They lay out an endless journey of empowerment ahead of us.

Growing up, we became inspired by what we could endure and what we could be despite our father. Paradoxically, the feelings of inferiority and incompetence that our father instilled in us led us to leverage the other component that he had accidentally constructed: our powerful determination to overcome our perceived weaknesses. In attempting to destroy us, our father provided us with exactly the tools and the power that we needed to overcome him. We learned not to react clumsily with our emotions, but instead to sceptically unpack everything that happened to us and learn from it. The things we lost in our struggles with our father only served to commit us to the fight. We wear our wounds with pride for they signify all that we were willing to sacrifice to live in opposition to evil.

It is normal and healthy to feel anger in response to evil. We will not be defeated by evil if we despise it. Evil is the forsaking of everything human. It chooses to stand against everything of meaning and to destroy everything of value. Evil is not a thing. It is a choice. Evil is the choice of the weak.

As Viktor E. Frankl said: 'An abnormal reaction to an abnormal situation is normal behaviour.'[2] The mental adaptions we made while trapped in such an aggressive environment were not pathological, but incredibly useful and ingenious adaptive traits that lent us the required resilience to survive. We learned to adjust our minds to whatever circumstances we encountered.

When we were burdened we maintained our posture so that it did not break our backs. When we sustained our balance, the struggles only made us stronger as our resilience was trained against enormous weight.

Women are often described as fragile but this is just another stereotype derived from patriarchal beliefs. Our mother and Charlotte were the two most determined and powerful individuals that we have ever known. It was so natural for our mother and sister to love and endure that we came to expect superhuman resilience from everyone we encountered. They gave us our strength and demonstrated that it is not inevitable that encountering evil will riddle us with hatred, but instead will teach us the value of love.

Often, it is understood that being good excludes optionality in life and is defined by what 'cannot be done'. But our father's behaviour negated any possibility that he could love. Evil excludes good by polluting our entire existence with hatred which will crowd out any possibilities for love, beauty and joy. The only thing that good excludes is the possibility of evil.

Morality is sometimes construed as restrictive and consisting of an authority responsible for the governing rules of our lives. This was the lie of morality that our father tried to force upon us. A different conception of morality that we learned from our mother and sister is based on our self-interest in bettering our character and pursuing virtues. This morality is found in the idiosyncrasy of each circumstance, its nuanced context and the decisions that we make. We have learned that true morality must exist on the level of the individual for everyone to create for themselves. Anyone who claims, as our father did, that they have a moral system which obliges others to conform is simply an oppressor.

Only when we respect our own lives do we have a stake in the world. Altruism unfortunately is a very hard concept to scale authentically and it is subject to many forms of corrupting narcissism and power games. Abusers will often praise their own 'altruism' which is impossible to interpret without knowing their intentions. Our father would even praise himself for not hitting our mother as 'other men would' as if we owed him for such 'sacrifices'.

Evil is born from the relinquishing of our responsibility in the world. Therefore, enlightened self-interest is the only way to ensure that we are all grounded and invested in each other's and the world's continued success.

Our father spent his entire life attempting to force his misogynistic and hateful values upon us. We are testament to the fact that values cannot be forced onto others;

this is never an excuse. Our strength forever lies in our choices to create our own moral codes. If we do not think for ourselves then we will attempt to find comfort in rules, through either conformism or totalitarianism: this is the abuser's goal.

Suffering under our father led us to search desperately for an objective morality that we could hold him to account against. We wished we could control his actions with a rock-solid intellectual foundation to support us. Yet, this was simply the urge of resorting to tyranny to revolt against a tyrant.

When confronted with so much evil and feeling its devastating effects, the question is often raised: 'Why be good?' The answer is that goodness is a state of being that is desirable in itself.

A morality that strives towards virtue benefits us individually. Where we strive to be good, we do not need to believe in the goodness or fairness of the world; it only requires that we believe in ourselves. Pursuing virtue is an act of freedom and self-development. It is not the freedom to follow our emotions, but freedom from our emotions. It is developing beyond a simple determinism where we are puppets to stimuli and regress into the 'instinctive man', but instead become something greater. It is the freedom to be defined by the values that we choose. We understand our emotions and what they are telling us; however, we choose not to be obliged to follow their capricious nature.

The conception of morality that we learned from our mother and sister means that we have a duty to first look after ourselves before we can help others, otherwise we risk hurling ourselves into the world as a burden. This reliance on the world would make us fragile and dependent on circumstance. Our character is the only thing that persists; everything else can be taken from us.

To overcome suffering, we have learned that it is key to internalise our goals; to focus on our character. External goals are guesses at possibilities that we have no control over. External success should only be epiphenomenal and occur as secondary to the development of our character. This is what we have learned from our success in the world as a result of those internal struggles which demanded our attention.

It is sometimes difficult for us not to lust after the external world; however, this will never satisfy us. We observed in our father that an oppressor requires the oppressed. He will seek them out with all his energy. His power is as vulnerable as the downtrodden. An oppressor without the oppressed is simply an insecure wreck who has no internal strength and must pursue this externally.

An obsession with control over the external world inevitably leads to internal delusion. Our father valued his own interpretation of events above reality and it's clear that if each person tried to shape the world in their image, the world would look like no one and would lie in ruins. It's clear that our father projected himself into the world to escape himself.

Our trauma will not be overcome by attempting to answer the vacillating and emotionally loaded questions which arise in our minds. The basic axioms of our belief systems can only be attained from life itself. We are finding safety in leaps of faith, throwing ourselves into the plain acts of living.

It can be incredibly hard to discard unhelpful beliefs. However, from our new bare perspective, we are building ourselves back with the full awareness we have gained from the traumatic events that we have suffered. This is an opportunity to build life on the most solid foundations.

We are learning to approach this new world of ours with curiosity. Doubt is uncomfortable but certainty is foolish. The most important job of those who search for truth is to destroy false certainties. We will use our new perspective to tackle the corrupt rationalisations we observed in the treatment of our family's tragedy.

Collectively, we have a responsibility to challenge one another's beliefs and to constantly search for truth. If we refuse to talk about issues like domestic abuse, we allow dangerous views to live beyond our periphery. Only when we have open and honest public conversations is the truth of each side of every argument revealed. Only then are dangerous beliefs legitimately destroyed.

Conflict is inherent in the structure of the world; each dialectic that cannot resolve itself will build stronger opposites until the inevitable confrontation. Therefore, we must always engage in conflict with evil and never turn away. In fact, it is not possible to ignore evil. If we attempt to restrict our consciousness and squeeze it from awareness this simply reduces our scope for living. Evil will persist, and we become blind and vulnerable.

Illusion can temporarily protect us from the harsh realities of life, but it simply forces more illusion as we allow our conditions to deteriorate. Wherever we suffer in silence, we condemn not only ourselves but everyone suffering in the same way. The goal of the abusers is to alienate their victims and to ensure they suffer in silence. Collectively, we must not facilitate this.

We must ensure that abusers have to look over their shoulders, feel uneasy about their behaviour and worry that their closed doors will offer them no protection. There are two possible worlds we can choose between. One, where good people fear those who are evil, which is unfortunately the world that we currently live in. The other, where evil people fear those who are good. This is the world we wish to create.

Therefore, we need to change the standards of acceptable behaviour within the homes in our country. Currently many accept abuse as part of life and that is often why there is a failure of the abused to identify the injustice they are suffering.

Stories of suffering function for society like the mechanisms of pain in the body; they teach the organism that it needs to act or cease carrying on as it is. To overcome damaging beliefs we must be willing to communicate our struggles. We mustn't allow our experiences to become stagnant and the opportunities that they possess to be lost.

We, as a society, must not ignore those messages of pain. Our story demonstrates the consequences of ignoring the messages our body is conveying.

Flashback – Top Dog

RYAN

It's a Friday night and I've just landed into London City airport, collected my bag and I'm trying to get home as quickly as I can. It's a frequent journey for me; every weekend in fact.

I'm so excited to be home for another weekend. I'm twenty-five years old, yet my favourite times are spent with my three dogs, my mum and my little sister. I honestly couldn't think of anything else I'd rather do.

The train pulls into the London City airport terminal and I jump on. I switch SIM cards in my phone, from the Dutch SIM for work to my UK SIM for the weekends.

My phone is now buzzing with all the messages and missed calls from the past week. Usually, the missed calls and messages are from cold callers, but now, unusually, I can see multiple missed calls from my father. If at all possible, I avoid speaking to him and we certainly never contact each other's mobiles.

'I'm trying to get hold of you. I have bad news. Call me back,' one of the messages reads.

I message Mum on Facebook. 'Hi Mum. Dad left me a message saying there is bad news. Do I want to know now what it is?'

'Don't worry. I will tell you when you get home,' Mum replies.

'Is it bad? Why would Dad call me? I need to know, is Max OK? Yes or no.'

Max is our fifteen-year-old Yorkshire terrier. He is healthy and vibrant, but I am always worried for him because our father displays no concern for his wellbeing and often treats him as an inconvenience.

'No,' Mum writes back. At that moment I knew Max would be in pain. Only recently, he was rushed to the vet by Charlotte as our father outright refused to take Max, believing he wasn't worth the money any more.

I knew that if anything had happened to Max, our father would leave him to suffer at home, rather than pay for help from a vet. I message Mum to tell her to do everything she can to help Max, and that I will pay for any vet bills.

'Just up here on the left. The gravel drive with the silver car.'

The taxi pulls up to the house. I push the front door open and look Mum in the eyes. I instantly know. I rush inside, into her arms and we both start crying.

In stark contrast to our grief, our father is standing next to us. He is repeatedly telling me how he found Max dead, with a sadistic smile on his sick face. He is enjoying this emotional power over us.

'The dog is dead. I kicked the bed and it didn't move,' he muttered, emotionless.

I pull Mum away and we walk to grieve and comfort each other in a different room, but my father continues to follow us.

'I'll bury it in the garden,' he grumbles.

'Leave us alone!' I yell, and Mum and I head outside.

'What happened?' I ask, wiping the tears from my face.

'Charlotte was playing with Max at lunchtime before she left, then your father came back for lunch. Charlotte said there was absolutely nothing wrong with Max, he was running around the house and bounding with energy. An hour after Charlotte left I came back from work and Max was dead. Your father was stood over him just poking him and shaking the bed. He responded exactly the same to me as he did to you just then.'

How did this happen?

Max was always the man of the house, we certainly looked up to him more than we did our father. Our father wouldn't have killed a dog, surely? It couldn't be. No one's masculinity is so fragile that they are threatened by a small dog.

Is it?

5

OUR MEANING

'Man is what he wills himself to be.'

Jean-Paul Sartre

The Meaning We Lost

We idolised our mother, Claire, and sister, Charlotte. Their perseverance always inspired us to keep going. They lived through their actions of kindness and enlightened self-sacrifice. They shared endless love where they saw vulnerability. They taught us that the greatest individuals are not those with the highest ideals, but those who live each day with the purest actions.

It is from them that we are forged. It is their love that protected us from the oppressive hate of our father. It was their spirit which gave us hope. They showed us that, despite an environment so destructive, we can always choose life and love.

Their strength demonstrated to us that cruelty is derived from weakness. It takes strength and courage to remain engaged in a battle for good despite knowing the suffering that it can bring upon us. Our father demonstrated that cruelty is derived from the incapacity to endure life. Life breaks many without them realising. It takes perseverance to sustain life. To give up living is to become death in this world.

We always knew we were surrounded by two angels. They taught us to appreciate the simple things in life. They taught us compassion where as two young boys we had seen only competition.

Mum and Charlotte were selfless, caring people. They both loved animals and loved to spoil our dogs. Charlotte loved horse riding and volunteered with the elderly and the disabled. She was sporty and adventurous. Our mother and Charlotte were almost like sisters: they would escape to Charlotte's room together to do each other's makeup and watch movies.

It wasn't until Charlotte joined our lives that we truly learned to appreciate the softness of life and its wonderful beauty. As young boys, we had simply considered ourselves and everything around us to be indestructible. We charged around and spent our days play-fighting. When Charlotte arrived, we became so careful and gentle around her, as if we were walking upon thin ice. However, it wasn't long until she was tougher than us. Charlotte taught us the courage that it takes to live life on its own terms in total vulnerability. We felt our shells and boyish brinkmanship melt away in her presence.

Charlotte's blue eyes and blonde hair lit up our lives like sunshine. She became a mirror image of our mother before she had even learned to speak. From the moment she could support herself on her own two feet, Charlotte wished to care for everything and never tired. Loving gave her endurance. Love was her fuel, her reward and her gift to the world. Charlotte lived to love. Those two words were inseparable to her.

Having grown up with two brothers, Charlotte developed an impressive juxtaposition of beauty and boisterousness. One day she could be dressed up in high heels and partying until the early hours of the morning and on another she'd be sprawled on the floor with pizza, playing on our Xbox and scolding 'camping noobs' through the headset.

Charlotte was an intrepid adventurer with a wild adventurous streak. In 2015 she travelled halfway around the world to visit Ryan in Australia. For the first week of her three-week trip, Ryan was working on a drilling rig in the Australian outback. Charlotte relished the opportunity to explore Brisbane by herself. Having grown up in small villages in rural Cambridgeshire and Lincolnshire, Charlotte leapt into this new freedom with an unleashed enthusiasm. Charlotte crammed her trip with rock climbing, surfing, white-water rafting, hiking, snorkelling, paddle-boarding and kayaking to name only a few activities. It was a trip that defined Charlotte as she overcame many fears.

It was her first time rock climbing even though she had always suffered from a paralysing fear of heights. On the trip, Charlotte stood with trepidation, gazing from the bottom of the 20-metre-high outdoor Kangaroo Point cliffs. Charlotte began clambering and contorting herself to meander up this intimidating wall. She fought to rise to this symbol of her own elevation, this vast partition between her fear and freedom. Eventually, as the fatigue wore her down and Charlotte was not sure if she could ascend any further, Ryan came across and explained that she had done a fantastic job to get where she was but, unfortunately, she had another 19.5 metres to go. One hour later and Charlotte had made it to the top. Once she had abseiled back down to the bottom, she was overcome with relief. The fear was purged from her as she cried and laughed at the same time, eyes streaming but also snot stringing from her nostrils as she gasped for air in between her cry-laughs.

Obviously, Charlotte needed energy to sustain her passion for adventure. This huge demand for fuel was met with her love of food, in particular chocolate. Often, Charlotte would be plagued with the difficulty: 'I want chocolate, but I don't know which form.' With cheeks stuffed with whatever chocolate she could find and a satisfied expression, she would exclaim: 'It's like magic in my mouth!'

The one thing that Charlotte loved more than chocolate was animals. Despite being allergic to animal hair for much of her younger years, she would knock back an antihistamine and throw herself into snuggles and cuddles with whatever animals happened to be nearby. She had the ability to communicate with animals as if she spoke the multitude of barks, whistles and chirps as naturally as English. Charlotte would spend countless hours playing with the dogs in the garden, teaching them tricks and taking them on walks around the woods or to the beach. Some of the happiest times of her life were spent with them. She always joked that she would have a thousand rescue dogs when she was older (and it was difficult to know whether she was actually joking).

When Charlotte was with her friends she was never afraid to make a fool of herself to make others laugh. After completing her A levels, she went on holiday with her friends to Salou in Spain. On arrival and bristling with excitement, she immediately sang 'Uptown Funk' at the top of her voice on the balcony as pedestrians looked on.

One prominent memory that sticks in our minds was during a school quiz when Charlotte was certain that she knew the answer to a question on swimming technique. The answer happened to be 'doggy paddle' and in her eagerness, at the top of her voice, Charlotte simply screamed the words 'doggy style!' Charlotte wasn't afraid of sharing the story with anyone she met and enjoyed laughing at her own misfortune.

Our mother was our foundation. She was always there. She was as ever-present as the air we breathed. She was the hidden mechanism behind everything that happened in our lives.

Our mother was our cheerleader. She believed in our capacity to achieve anything. She gave us rocket boosters. She gave us everything she could and what we had was all that we could have ever wished for. She charged our batteries to last us for lifetimes.

Our mother was our medicine. She would always ask how we were, not in a phatic way, but with bottomless interest. She wouldn't allow us to not look after ourselves.

She was so full of love that it cascaded down from her like the warmth from the sun.

Our mother was the antidote to our father. She showed us that we were valuable, capable and good despite our father's insistence otherwise. She was the stoic symbol of strength which stood in response to the weakness and vicious vacillations of our father. Her tireless caring enabled us to have the opportunities to succeed and we always endeavoured to fill our mother's life with happiness and a sense of pride.

Growing up, our mother's deteriorating multiple sclerosis troubled us, and we always tried to create a calm environment for her. Exercise also helped her slow the progression of the illness and we therefore encouraged our mother to take up swimming. She took to it naturally. It taught her that she could learn new skills and to believe in herself again, something our father had long ago stolen. Swimming became the source of our mother's freedom and was the place where she enjoyed peace.

However, the biggest challenge for our mother was finding the time to swim once she was in the pool. She was such an approachable and friendly person that it was inevitable that she would make many friends in this new environment. Most of the swimming sessions were spent chatting with fellow swimmers, almost always about her children.

The Castle Sports swimming pool soon became a place of refuge for us all; for peace and for socialising. For many, one hour a week swimming would be an insignificant activity but for us it was a luxury. It was not without significant resistance and consistent conflict from our father that we achieved this small victory.

With every breath, our mother and Charlotte immersed themselves in life. They lived for the only thing that truly matters: caring for the creatures on our Earth.

Our mother and Charlotte were created perfectly for this world. It was impossible to tell whether they created it, or it created them. Certainly, they created our world with their own hands.

Flashback – Locked Inside

RYAN

'He's taken every penny out of my purse, and from the joint account. I have no money at all. What am I going to do, Ryan?' Mum pleads on the phone.

'Mum, don't worry. I'll transfer over whatever money you need. We'll figure this out. Try not to worry about the money. Luke and I will look after you and Charlotte.'

'He hasn't said where he's gone. I've just gotten an email from him saying he will ration back enough for me to pay the bills, and that's all.'

I can hear the anger, confusion and worry in my mum's voice. She worked tirelessly every day to support us, and this morning our father disappeared with everything. Any hope we have to break Mum and Charlotte free to start a new life has vanished along with the money he took. Without the savings, Luke and I will need to find even more money to get our mother and sister free.

'Mum, calm down! We'll get you the money you need. We'll sort this out. Just keep me informed of what happens. Lock the doors and, whatever you do, do not open the doors for him! In fact, change the locks now! Don't let him back in the house until I'm back home this weekend! I love you, Mum.'

Mum puts the phone down and heaves a deep sigh.

There is a knock at the door and Mum and Charlotte freeze.

'Come on, let me in! I love you. Stop being silly and open the door!' pleads our father.

The front door is locked. Charlotte and Mum are inside, terrified. Our father monologues outside with glib apologies and promises, all of which he has broken a hundred times before.

Our mother, as if an empty shell, begins to walk slowly towards the door, transfixed, unsure even of what she will do.

'Mum, get away from the door! Do not let him in! What are you doing?' Charlotte screams as our mum edges towards the front door.

As if she is possessed, Mum hears nothing around her.

'Stop it, Mum!' cries Charlotte as our mother slowly turns the mechanism, retracting the iron bolts back within the doorframe.

As the bolt springs back with a click, there is a moment of heavy silence.

Our mother suddenly realises what she has done and

steps back quickly to stand with Charlotte at the end of the hallway.

Our father pushes the door with a dissembling softness, and it slowly creaks open.

A solid line of light streams through the doorway, passing across the wall of the hallway, illuminating pictures of our childhood and the smiling faces of ignorant youth. The light rushes towards our mum and sister, standing motionless at the end of the hallway, gazing ahead with fixed eyes. Both are staring at the doorway, the line where he changes. The disconnect between the outside and inside. The doorway between different worlds.

The opening door reveals our father's silhouette, with the bright light streaming from behind.

He remains standing on the other side of the entrance. He is grinning with unsettling facial twitches betraying his apparently conciliatory tone, indicating a face unused to such alien expressions.

It is reminiscent of a clown, a caricature of human emotion. A clown that others outside found amusing, but past that line, into the house, was a clown from a horror film which filled us with fear.

'I've brought back our money, dear.'

He steps over the line, and in that moment they feel him change. He walks slowly towards them both.

Mum and Charlotte shuffle back until they bump into the kitchen counter with nowhere to go. He continues with a more disturbing smile now. His face looks as if it is slowly unravelling, his true character beginning to tear through his flimsy reputation. The mask he wears to show the world is dissolving away the further he comes inside.

'What's going on? I love you guys. Why would you lock the doors? Come here and give me a hug!' His voice flutters between an eerie calmness and punctuated intensity, as if he is mutating.

This change in behaviour is frightening, but not unusual.

'What on earth are you doing? You disappeared with everything and then rationed me barely enough to pay the bills. Now you just turn up out of the blue and ask for a hug?!' our mum cries.

'Dad, fuck off!' Charlotte bravely bellows.

'Look, your mother can't be trusted with money. I had to do this in order to protect the money for your university fees, Charlotte. And Claire, I'm looking after the money so that we can pay for your multiple sclerosis treatment. I'm going to give you access to the online bank accounts. Not many men would allow their wives this much freedom, but I'm different, I love you. I love my family.'

Our father is ignoring Charlotte entirely and looking directly at our mother; he knows Charlotte cannot be persuaded this time. She is fuming as our father continues to plead for forgiveness.

His face is now trembling as he attempts to maintain this façade; his emaciated smile is struggling to remain propped up by atrophied muscles he never uses except as a last resort.

'I shouldn't have disappeared like that. It won't happen again. I promise.'

It no longer matters what he says; he's back inside, and he knows it.

His expression regresses to his usual scowl, and very soon, so will his behaviour.

Finding Meaning in Suffering

It was nine months after our family tragedy. Ryan had left the country. He was away working for a month and it was his birthday on 22 April 2017, a few days after he had left. We had both begun to stumble into our new life. We had achieved a base level of functioning, but were still dazed and trying to find our feet.

Luke chose to write a letter to Ryan to talk honestly about what had happened. It was time to engage with the past and begin to unravel it together. We needed to find out where our lives now pointed us. We needed to be our own guidance.

To build our lives on solid foundations we had to scrape through our past and our emotions to tear out everything that no longer served us.

After the endless media commentary on our tragedy it was also time that we told our side of the story. We needed to be comfortable to talk about our life. We had witnessed the societal reticence that constrains action on domestic abuse and we weren't willing to let ourselves become so afraid to talk that we perpetuated this silence. We had a heavy responsibility to share our experience.

The rest of our lives held three possibilities: a life consumed with bitterness, a life of detachment and paralysing fear of the emotional storms within us, or we could open up with honest vulnerability, the idea of which petrified us.

Despite the pain that we'd been through, we had to begin a life of vulnerability and honesty that we had no idea how to navigate. We would live terrified, but for once we had the ability to choose the challenges that terrified us.

To demonstrate his commitment to these values, Luke chose to post his letter to Ryan on Facebook, hoping that the response would empower Ryan to talk if he ever needed to.

The most powerful commitments in life are gestures of complete vulnerability; simple human kindness with no guarantee of return. Despite this, being truly honest was always our greatest fear in life. We had spent our lives learning to conceal our emotions.

If we truly wanted to feel safe we had to throw ourselves into danger to realise that we could handle it. We held onto feelings of despair because the only way to let them out was to feel them. Now our father was gone, we had to learn that we would support each other through this.

Prior to writing this letter, we'd never been able to explicitly tell each other anything that we'd appreciated before. We'd learned an invisible appreciation, something our father would never pick up on. We would always talk to others about how proud we were of our mother and siblings but never could say the words to each other's faces. How insignificant our fear seems now.

The following is the open letter Luke penned to Ryan:

What I've written below is something that I've never been able to say and probably never will be able to say in person to my little brother, Ryan.

212

On 19 July 2016 our father shot and killed our mum, Claire, and our nineteen-year-old sister, Charlotte. It was the result of decades of abuse and controlling and intimidating behaviour. He was a tyrant who wouldn't let his family live outside of his domination. Our father was a terrorist living within our own home; he had no cause but to frighten his family and to generate his own esteem from trampling and bullying us. For over a decade, we had tried to leave on numerous occasions, but he manipulated and threatened us every time.

Ever since we were young boys, Ryan and I aspired to a better life for Mum and Charlotte and to finally give our family the life our father had deprived us of. Ryan and I had been working abroad since leaving university and had raised enough money to rent a small place for Charlotte and Mum while we saved to find a place elsewhere for them. We moved Mum out of our house while our father was out, only a few days before the event on 19 July 2016. Killing our mother and sister was our father's final denial of the future we had spent our lives trying to create for Mum and Charlotte, the life that they deserved. He killed himself in an act of cowardice, finally showing how little he had to live for outside of punishing his family for his own distorted sense of power.

Leading up to the event on 19 July, I had always believed I was the strong, older brother. I had always tried to put on a brave face and attempted to defuse the tensions of our father, doing my best to calm the environment. However, after university, Ryan and I moved away from home for work and our father's behaviour deteriorated further. The effects were becoming unmanageable for me. Charlotte was suffering from severe depression and suicidal thoughts and had dropped out of university. Mum's multiple sclerosis was deteriorating rapidly from the stress our father was causing her and she was taking prescribed morphine every day to dampen the pain that her disease inflicted.

I could no longer face going home because I didn't know what I could do any more; I didn't feel I could manage, I felt entirely helpless. I was overwhelmed. Ryan had always come home every weekend that he could. At the time, he was working in Holland and made the journey home every weekend to check that Mum and Charlotte were OK and to resist our father's behaviour. He would always look after Mum and Charlotte and spent his money on them rather than himself. Whether it was for Charlotte to come on holiday to visit him when he was working in Australia or for swimming lessons for Mum, he always gave them a powerful optimism in what was a despairing situation for us all.

Since 19 July last year, it's become clear to me that I wouldn't be here without my little brother. I act strong, but he is strong. Even when we struggled through our darkest moments against our father, Ryan dared to remain resistant when I had broken down and couldn't face any more. He was still able to love and believe in a world that our father had filled with hate. Ryan's resilience and hope were perceived by our father as a rebuttal of his dominance. For that Ryan suffered the strongest wrath from our father. Throughout it all, I had shut my emotions down because I simply didn't have the courage to confront the reality of our situation; I became more detached and hidden within myself to diminish the trauma. Ryan protected us; he never hid but always threw himself in the firing line to shield us.

Nothing can ever replace what we lost on 19 July and no words can describe what we have endured. Every day, I still feel the panic and scramble for the reset button, struggling with the feeling that, somehow, we live in the wrong world. For the rest of our lives, we must learn to deal with what happened on that day.

The last year has drawn into focus how lucky we all were to have Ryan. I remember when I was with Charlotte and she would only talk of how proud she was to have a brother like Ryan. No mother could hope for a better son, so determined to love his mother no matter what storms it brought him. I often think that Ryan is exactly the kind of man that the world needs more of.

We now live together with our dogs, Indi and Bella, who Mum and Charlotte gave so much love and attention to. Ryan currently works abroad, and I know that in the future he would love to be able to spend more time with the dogs. If the dogs are happy, then Ryan is happy, and if Ryan is happy then I'm happy.

For all that we've been through, there isn't much I can give Ryan to show my appreciation. It's his determination that has kept me going, minute by minute, hour by hour and day by day for twenty-six years and for that I honestly owe him my life. I couldn't have fought the battles by myself and towards the end the battles had beaten me, but not him. He is indestructible; a force for good that cannot be stopped. He is the person I've needed to stand up for me when I am too weak. For everything our father has done to attempt to destroy Ryan, he has failed. Ryan is the strongest, most kind-hearted person and refuses to let the hate triumph over the love he fought for. I've piggybacked on his strength for all these years. Ryan refuses to give up fighting for something better, he stares hard-nosed into the face of cruelty and he always finds hope when everything seems futile.

I have started this fundraising page because I want Ryan to know that I care, and I want him to know that other people care too. I could never say what I've said above to his face; in fact, even if I tried, I'm sure he'd punch me. I want Ryan to be able to follow his dreams in life; he doesn't deserve the struggles that he's faced. I want him to believe that good things can happen and to believe in the future that lies ahead of him. As we spend the rest of our lives rebuilding, as we look to find new things to believe in, new hope and new meaning, I want him to be free to be whoever he wants to be, the person he deserves to be. I don't think Mum and Charlotte could be prouder of him now; if they were looking down I'm sure they'd have tears in their eyes as they wonder what on earth he is made of. I'm certain that evil is haunted by nightmares of my little brother.

It's Ryan's twenty-sixth birthday on 22 April and

I want to wish him the best future that he could ever hope for; I hope you can join me.

My little brother is my hero and I love him.

We had to acknowledge that to live is to suffer and that to live well is to find meaning in that suffering; as Nietzsche said, 'He who has a why to live can bear almost any how.'[1] We could not hide from the suffering we had endured for our lives. Now we had acknowledged it, we had to learn to overcome it.

Suffering presents meaning in its challenge to us. As with all things of difficulty it cannot destroy us without also offering us the possibility to become stronger.

When we find the meaning within our suffering we are met with the responsibility to act on that meaning, otherwise we will be struck down with guilt. This is articulated by Dostoevsky who said, 'There is only one thing that I dread: not to be worthy of my sufferings.'[2]

We cannot create meaning separate from our circumstances. Life draws us into confrontations and challenges that we must turn to and face. It is important to turn and face suffering otherwise we never learn how to overcome it, but will instead learn to fear it. We cannot create our own meaning disconnected from the callings of our circumstances. We are defined by how we respond to our circumstances. Decisions, not conditions, define us.

As a superhero does not exist without a villain, meaning does not exist without problems. It does not matter what we expect from life but what life expects from us. What a shame that so many of us spend so long running away from exactly the things which would give our lives meaning. The problem of problems never goes away. Therefore, we must find a problem that we are willing to spend our entire lives solving. For us, that problem is tackling male violence against women and children.

Flashback – Safe as Houses

The safe door clunks shut as our father returns our mother's life savings to the metal box.

Mum looks around, with a gasp. She sees the safe chained up to a series of bars in the garage. Inside is her identity: her passport, her driver's licence, her birth certificate and all £15,000 of her life's savings.

Only yesterday, he had returned with her money and insisted that he would allow her freedom over her finances. He insisted he would change. It was a ruse. It's always a ruse. He wanted to chip away the next level of freedom and he has succeeded, again.

His arms are folded and he smirks contentedly. He is no longer begging and pleading as he was yesterday; he now stands with a disturbing pride.

Our mother's shadow, always following her and threatening her, he now casts darkness over her.

The chains are strewn across the garage like a giant spider's web in which she is entangled. It is all so invisible to the outside, yet she feels as if she is physically handcuffed. The safe door is locked shut, yet the door everyone else sees to the house looks as open and inviting as any other.

She feels anchored to this safe, like a helpless fly caught in our father's web.

'Let's go and watch TV, shall we?' our father carelessly mutters as he wanders back into the house.

Our mother stands transfixed. She feels she cannot move, as if she were entwined in the chains. How far can she really go? She may as well be in that safe.

In fact, she realises that she always has been.

She suddenly sees how he managed to do it for so long. How he managed to beat her down without his fists, how he managed to isolate her without a prison and how he managed to silence her without a gag.

At last, with the safe in front of her, she sees the intangible reality which had always escaped her, always imprisoned her. He thinks he's won. But now, she sees the truth. The truth is chained right in front of her eyes. She sees her enemy. Finally, she knows how he does it, how he stole her life so effortlessly.

Now, at last, she knows how to break free.

6

OUR LIGHT

'Very little is needed to make a happy life.'

Marcus Aurelius

Fanning the Embers

In the days and months following our tragedy, we were incredibly lucky to have so many kind individuals around us for support. Everyone treated us with compassion and were careful to give us the space and time to be alone, while also offering a hand and basic care if needed. We savoured moments of serenity when we could sit down at a dinner table with home-cooked food and warm, smiling faces.

After a lifetime of self-alienation, we had to admit that we needed others to help soften us from the harsh blow we had taken. Our initial reaction to such horrific trauma was to double up efforts to rebuild our personal shells. However, while we stumbled around, hurriedly attempting to pick up the fragments, we realised that others were not here to finish us off. We slowly began to ease into this naked and honest existence.

It will take years to bleed our systems of the emotional remnants from our father's actions. However, there is no reason for us to hold onto this pain and there is certainly no reason for us to act in service of it. Our task is to overcome it where we can through our choices and to let our bodies handle the rest of the slow healing process.

Significant introspection was required to unearth the source of deep emotions within us. Our emotions initially wanted to be expressed in the world, they desired targets. To understand the source of our emotions we had to learn to swim upriver until we found the true spring. This required enduring sickening pain until we could see what lay behind.

After we learned to honestly engage with our emotions, we then required the gentle love of those around us to ease us back into the world, slowly and supportively.

Whether it was friends from decades ago, or dog walkers we met after the murders, we only encountered kindness. Within the community we were offered the opportunity to respect and remember our mother and sister through memorials at the Spalding High School, Morrisons, where our mother worked, and the charity that our sister and mother loved to donate to: Wood Green animal shelters. We were honoured that the community wished to pay their respects to our mother and sister. It struck us just how many lives they had touched.

These acts of compassion helped us to feel that our grief was shared. We felt understood and less alone knowing that our mother and sister were also on the minds of those kind individuals. We could feel their arms around us and that they wanted us to grow out of this moment; we felt them willing us on.

It was during the preparation of the memorials for our mother and sister that we began to feel our hearts warming. It gave us time to breathe and to reflect on all that had come before. It gave us an understanding of the larger family of humanity and the deep love that we can all muster for others who are in a crisis. These moments of deep honesty and vulnerability with others showed us a side of human interaction so often missing except in times of unbearable grief. We felt the community collectively take up the responsibility to carefully rehabilitate us.

We were helped beyond any obligations by members of every part of the community; even the smallest actions had enormous positive effects on us. There are too many cases to list, but instances include the vet providing free treatment as we were getting through the difficulties of learning to look after our two dogs, the kind donation of the trees for the memorials and even being encouraged back to the Castle Sports gym and swimming pool, where our mother and sister had been murdered. When we began to lose our balance, there was always a friendly hand to stabilise us.

It was the aggregation of these disparate, uncoordinated, kind acts that helped us to recalibrate. We learned to adapt from a world of tyranny, fear and manipulation to one where we could, at least momentarily, relax and for once get to know ourselves and those around us honestly.

Simple kindness is the most powerful antidote to life's tragedies. Working so hard and losing so much destroys the entire foundation of your life. It destroys motivation for doing anything at all. It steals meaning from everything. Kindness provided the soft landing and the trampoline to bounce us back up again. We were shown that there was new meaning to be found in the world.

Alongside all those who have stood by us to guide us back into the world, we have both found the kindness of our dogs to be the most powerful source of our capacity to love and care. Life comes naturally to animals and it is impossible not to be carried by their momentum. Indi and Bella have brought smiles to our faces every single day. They teach us unbounded love that we find impossible not to reciprocate.

Throughout the evil and ignorance that we have experienced, we have always been more struck by the greater potential for good in the human heart. Despite the world's violence and cruelty, there are those silent heroes who triumph over the propagation of evil, who refuse to be its host and proliferate it further. Unchecked, and without huge expenditures of energy, evil would consume everything. Our own response and that of those around us has given us hope that good cannot be destroyed by evil, but evil certainly can be destroyed by good.

Sometimes life presents us with a limited hand where none of the choices available to us are those we would wish to make. We've learned that in these circumstances we must simply choose the least bad option and slow our descent until a time comes when we are able to grow out of our circumstances. We must be happy with a life that is good enough and never resort to resentfulness or this slow decline will become a slippery and deep descent.

Our lives look very different now. Both of us have always been highly competitive. Ryan, younger by one-and-a-half years, has always pushed Luke to his limit to maintain relevance as an older brother. Ryan is the type of little brother who decides one day that he's going to jump out of aeroplanes. Luke is the kind of big brother who realises his little brother is jumping out of an aeroplane, so jumps out of an aeroplane simply to keep up. Every small victory is tallied to be recounted years later as a riposte to an even older micro-victory. We have always fed off each other and driven each other to succeed. However, despite our successes externally we had been harbouring a destitute inner life, a life we never showed to each other or spoke about but were now forced to confront.

We had learned to endure the insidious corrosivity of life under our father by leveraging our internal strength, but suddenly we had our worst nightmare thrust upon us. No amount of strength can withstand such brutality.

We had to find a way to navigate our way out, together. We had to support each other and find a new life, one that would now be empty of everything we had cared most about. We had to face dark and despairing questions while learning to live together. We both had to learn a tactfulness and sensitivity that we had little practice with.

We probably wouldn't have scored highly on domestic compatibility in ordinary circumstances. The last time that we had to do anything constructive together was probably a decade earlier and that would have been deciding who did the washing and who dried up. Now we were cramped into the tiny rental house we had secured for our mother and sister, where we didn't have our own space to be by ourselves. Two fiercely independent brothers, we now lived on top of each other.

Our tradition of competition was discarded as we both realised we barely had the capability to manage each day. We had to approach life's smallest challenges on our knees.

We realised that resentment would never teach us what we needed to learn to get out of where we were stuck. We had to ignore the entire world and we had to focus entirely on ourselves and each other. Our lives centred on each next step. We knew a mountain stood before us, but we didn't dare look up, we couldn't. We didn't have the capabilities to scale it and we didn't know where we would find them.

For the first few weeks we entirely relied on others to navigate for us. We were ferried from point to point and we simply did what was required of us. Dazed and disoriented, we felt unaccustomed to this strange town that was apparently our home.

We stared into the world as if it wasn't our own. Our minds couldn't understand our place within the world or how it functioned any more. Even the most basic comprehension escaped us.

Our days were simply spent waiting for a succinct and commanding text message from the police family liaison officers telling us the time that we would be picked up and what the next few hours held for us, primarily recounting our family history. Populating the gaps between these events, we spent our time playing with our dogs.

We began attempting to plan the funeral for our mother and sister. This was something we knew absolutely nothing about and were guided by friends and the community. As difficult as it was to write the eulogies, this began our journey of processing what had happened. Before this, everything seemed like just a story. We had only encountered words; people telling us what had happened. The reality was in other people's faces, but it hadn't fully penetrated our minds. As we wrote the eulogies, it brought our mother and sister closer to us as we realised how much of us was made from them.

Once the funerals were over we had to gather our belongings and everything we wished to keep from the family home in Moulton. Despite our father's sycophantic pandering to the police, pleading with them not to break the door down, they had done an absolutely smashing job of obliterating the front door. It gave us a strange sense of satisfaction seeing the last trivial and idiotic concern of a murderer flagrantly disregarded. The smashed door was a metaphor for all that our father hoped to achieve destroyed. It's impossible to understand why anyone would, as their last wish before an act of incomprehensible violence, request that a door is not damaged. However, the creaking door and the fragments of wood scattered across the drive showed us that nothing our father aimed to achieve in his life would succeed; not his perpetual attempts to destroy our lives and not his feeble attempt to save that stupid fucking door.

So, we ferried back and forth to the house when we could muster the strength to do so. To begin with, every visit to our house was eerie and left a sick taste in our mouths. It's not possible to convey the choking atmosphere of walking around our family house in perfect silence, seeing the scattered pictures and the furniture that we were familiar with. Yet, knowing that this was where our father concocted his hate for us all and ultimately planned the murder of our mother and sister, the house felt like it was haunted by a ghost.

We stumbled around the house in our nihilistic state trying to determine which things we wanted to keep and had room for in the tiny and already cramped rental house. It's almost impossible, after losing your mother and sister in circumstances like we did, to consider anything valuable at all. We wandered around looking at everything but feeling that it was tainted somehow; worried that anything we forgot to bring, or brought that we shouldn't have, would leave us traumatised or racked with irresolvable regret.

Many things we couldn't keep simply because we didn't have space. We spent many hours dismantling and stacking our belongings to be sold on eBay or Gumtree. We dedicated certain rooms for charity shop items, others for things we had to throw away and others as waiting for collection.

We treated it all as two engineers in severe trauma would. We treated it mechanically and functionally. We moved through this world of disconcerting sentimentality as if we were solving a giant jigsaw puzzle; simply moving this piece here and that piece there.

We opened the garage and let anyone who wanted tools to come and take them. We gave away much of the equipment that our mother used in the vegetable garden. We threw most of our own belongings away where they could not be given to charity.

We only wanted to keep our mother's and Charlotte's items. Even then, we required tens of trips to pack everything into the back of the car for transport to the rental house.

While we were sorting through our belongings we also had to manage our way through a mire of administration in delirious grief. We were drowning in legal documents and entwined in a sea of signatures. Legalese doesn't mean much in ordinary times, let alone when words themselves feel like faint impressions compared to the devastating world of human agency that we were still reeling from.

The things that mattered most to us were the dogs. They were our grounding in the world and they gave everything in our lives context. We were filled with dread at the idea that our dogs would come to harm. To lose our dogs would have absolutely shattered us. They were our last link to home, our refuge. They are our family.

Fire and Rainbows

Our dogs had always been central to some of the most entertaining moments of our lives. When we were lost in ourselves, they always dragged us back into the world with their sloppy licks and playful antics.

For example, when we moved our mother into the rental house, we were busily moving furniture around when we came to the living room. Indi was suspended and tangled in the blinds. She always enjoys staring out of windows to watch the world go by, and occasionally barks at it too.

However, due to the unfamiliar surroundings she had managed to ensnare herself to the point where she gave up. When we came in she was simply waiting, limp, as she slowly rotated with a look of resignation on her face. Once we'd untangled her, she immediately jumped back up to look out of the window again.

There have been many moments where we have all shared a laugh but there have also been some where they scared us to our core.

On one walk, Bella, spooked by a couple of larger and more boisterous dogs, simply ran away. The other dogs, encouraged and entertaining this as a game, gave chase. Bella disappeared. We searched desperately for ten minutes in total despair, screaming her name at the top of our voices. In desperation, we ran home hoping that we would find her here. Luckily, she was cowering in front of the door. A wave of tearful relief washed over us. Somehow, she had managed to cross two main roads to get there.

On another occasion, after Ryan had left the UK for a month-long work stint, Bella began the equivalent of a hunger strike. After two days, she broke her fast by reaching onto the counters, opening the cupboards and eating everything she could get her paws on. Nuts were scattered all over the house; there were vegetables dotted in every location, including our beds. One lone, half-eaten energy bar sat on the kitchen floor. It happened to be the only raisin and chocolate bar we had, of which both ingredients are potentially deadly to dogs in very small doses. The dogs were rushed to the vet and were induced to vomit. As expected, innocent Indi hadn't eaten anything. Bella on the other hand threw up a three-course meal. She then had to be looked after overnight so that they could continue to evacuate her stomach and keep an eye on her. Luckily there was no long-term damage and boisterous Bella was returned just as we had left her.

However, one particularly worrying episode occurred after we had both come back from the gym. We opened the door expecting both dogs to burst out and jump all over us as usual. Bella came bounding out, but Indi trailed tentatively behind. She seemed to be limping on every foot, groaning and heaving herself towards us with wide, panicked eyes.

We immediately took Indi to the vet. The vet looked her over and gave her squeezes at focused spots with a thoughtful and solemn look on his face. Indi winced and looked at us with fear. The vet performed a blood test and we waited agonisingly for the results in the waiting room.

The vet called us in and placed Indi on the table in front of us. He moved his hands to her waist and looked up at us. 'I'm afraid the problem with Indi is . . .' He gave her a gentle squeeze and a warm, rancid smell filled the small room.

Indi needed a fart.

Her tail immediately began wagging and her tongue cheekily popped out.

Moments like these filled us with terror at the prospect that we could not look after anything: our family, our dogs or ourselves. This was the fear of our father creeping back into our minds. Despite this fear, we couldn't afford to feel sorry for ourselves. We had to keep learning and do our best to manage.

Our living arrangements evolved organically. We lived in the small valley between the boxes stacked high up against each wall. Luke had the double bed upstairs and shared this with Bella. Two road bikes were lined against the walls, boxes bordered the bed and any gaps were stuffed with teddy bears. At bedtime, Bella would take a running jump to clear the floor and reach the bed.

Ryan ended up with a cramped single bed, in the dining room, wedged between a tumble dryer, unpacked boxes and a keyboard, with Indi sleeping on the pillow. The sheets were supposed to be white, but they were never lighter than dark cream. Ryan's bed was the midday nap area for Indi and Bella and was never free of dog hair, soil or toys.

Despite what seemed like a destitute living environment, we quickly acclimatised. With a large park only a two-minute walk away, we would take the dogs for walks at every opportunity: frosty mornings, in deep snow, sunrises and sunsets, summer afternoons and windy and violent winter evenings. We would often go at night after we had purchased flashing collars for the dogs. We enjoyed watching the blinking lights chase each other across the darkness with the stars and moon lighting up the clear night sky above us.

Every moment we spent with the dogs was a bittersweet reminder of all the love our mother and sister had given to us and the dogs. It reminded us of the joy we occasionally managed to steal together. It was these moments more than any others that reminded us that we are our mother's sons and our sister's brothers.

We became expert dog walkers. Beyond this, however, our clumsy attempts to look after ourselves led us to marvel at our comic ineptitude.

In many ways our lives had distorted and contorted us. We learned to live in our minds rather than to practically engage in a world that often left us feeling wrong and condemned whatever we did. This detachment from the world meant that we were often clumsy and uncoordinated in routine tasks.

We stumbled around the rental house like two giants living in a dark and damp cave. It was only possible to move through the rooms in single file because of the cluttering of boxes. The low doorframes were a continual nuisance and often led to cursing in the morning as Luke (6 feet 8 inches) and Ryan (6 feet 3 inches) persistently head-butted them. They were even low enough that if Luke stood upright, he would crack his nose on them. Often, in a doomed attempt to duck, we simply charged headfirst into the doorframes before falling to the floor sputtering profanities.

Having never had the luxury of such items under our command before, the tumble dryer provided an uninterrupted battle with its many blocked filters that we couldn't figure out how to access. It always caught us off guard when the water collection vessel overflowed onto Ryan's bed because we'd forgotten to empty it. We always assumed that the other had probably done it at some point. However, with the consequences being concentrated primarily on Ryan's bed, the responsibility fell onto his lap, so to speak.

Mould was a problem which we both struggled with

but neither of us could muster a defence against. At the very moment we checked anything for mould, it would be there. This often persuaded us not to look, as if we created it by the very act of doing so. There was a pile of teddies in the corner of Luke's bedroom. After three months, Luke responsibly decided to do a spot check for mould. He looked under the teddies and found so much multi-coloured and multi-textured mould that it had elevated the teddies from the floor.

Almost as if we realised it was best not to look at our attempts at normality, we were content with living in ever-increasing darkness as, one by one, lightbulbs blew throughout the house. It frequently reached the point where we would be showering with the aid of bike lights and navigating around the house with the residual light from the bedroom upstairs.

How many engineers does it take to change a lightbulb? More than two.

Our reluctance to change the bulbs was born from Ryan's first attempt where he managed to pull the glass bulb from the metal screw. The gas in the bulb expanded and, with a bang, the projectile bulb shot across the room, narrowly missing him.

There were many moments where we would have been screamed at by our father and so we tensed in anticipation but realised there was only silence. Maybe it was this immense relief that made us laugh so hard as everything seemed to go wrong around us. In fact, we learned to enjoy each accidental mishap or destruction.

While preparing our home for sale, we were midway

through mowing the lawn, which had grown to fantastic heights, when black smoke plumes began to rise ominously from the lawnmower. A moment later flames licked around the fuel tank. We anticipated an explosion and immediately ran away. However, after a few minutes the anticipation of disaster had diminished and we each tentatively tried to persuade the other to move in and check while we peered cautiously from our hiding places. As the most expendable of the two of us, but still keeping his distance, Luke gathered up the hose and soaked the lawnmower in water until the flames died down. Meanwhile, a faint rainbow illuminated the spray among the faltering smog. It was a sight that broke through the mundanity and grief of our days and left us both in stitches, laughing on the floor.

We had so many boxes in the rental house that we had to stack them upon the kitchen counters. Therefore, it was on top of the washing machine, which was awkwardly shoved into the middle of the kitchen, that we prepared our meals. In our first few weeks, we seemed unable to cook anything without the hobs setting nearby items on fire. Often, Luke would be cooking and Ryan would calmly walk into the kitchen, pick up a flaming dish cloth right next to Luke and take it outside to hose down. Somehow, Luke was oblivious to the inferno raging around him.

Frequently, after preparing a meal we would load the washing machine and leave the kitchen, only to have to run back minutes later at the sound of plates and food, which we'd forgotten to remove, being thrown off the washing machine and crashing onto the floor.

After we had become cognisant of the potentially explosive combination of Luke's cooking and our cluttered belongings, we decided to put as much as we could into the small wooden shed in the garden.

Unfortunately, there was an old rusted lock on the shed door and we didn't have a key (or we'd lost it — we can't remember). To get around this, Ryan purchased a lock-picking set.

The first test of Ryan's newly acquired lock-picking techniques came when we visited the family home in Moulton. After bashing the door down, the police had mounted a thick wooden sheet to cover the shattered half of the door and locked it shut using a brand-new, industrial padlock. In a flash of felony, Ryan picked the lock within five seconds. Uplifted by his success, and oddly keen to share his newly acquired criminal techniques with the police, Ryan later attempted to pick the old, rusty lock on the rental house's shed. However, this rusty lock proved much more resistant to Ryan's lock-picking. We therefore resorted to more aggressive tactics.

Believing that we understood the inner workings of the lock perfectly, we marked up the lock where its key mechanisms were located. We then attempted to carefully drill through the lock to simply release the locking mechanism and grant ourselves access.

After grinding two drill bits, which started at nearly 20cm long, down to mere stubs, we began to realise the lock wasn't going to yield easily. Unfortunately, by this point the springs and mechanisms had fallen out despite it still remaining firmly locked. We had reached the point of no return.

After we had destroyed all our drill bits, the lock was now mainly air populated with interstitial metal. Yet, still it held. As if millions of years of evolution had never happened, we both began bashing the lock with whatever pieces of metal we could find around us. Eventually, the limp lock fell off and we limped off.

We had now managed to free up a little extra space in the rental house, but it wasn't long before we were accumulating large amounts of rubbish to compound the space issues we thought we'd resolved. We had managed to get perfectly out of sync with the collection schedule, diligently putting our rubbish out when it was recycling day and recycling on rubbish day. We couldn't understand what we were doing wrong; had we failed in bin-collecting etiquette? Maybe we hadn't put it clearly enough at the front of the house. Maybe there were too many bags and they refused to take any at all. We experimented with different ways of presenting our bags for collection for a few weeks, building up quite a stockpile of rubbish and recycling bags in the process. This continued until our incompetence cancelled out and we accidentally put the 'wrong' bag out and realised that it got collected.

Finally, after a year, Luke received a job offer in London. In preparation for the move, it seemed we weren't suddenly going to leave our mishaps behind. In what was to prove a futile optimistic flurry, Ryan purchased a motorbike which he fell off the very next day, ending in a trip to the hospital. Ryan also managed, through an elaborate gear change, intending to put the car into first gear, to reverse into the neighbour's car. This was followed by a wide-eyed look of 'I didn't do anything' as the neighbour's car alarm protested otherwise. All this despite, by almost every quantifiable measure, Luke being the worst driver by far.

Eventually, we arrived at the new rental house in London. Once there, Luke had the simple task of assembling Ryan's second-hand bed which we had purchased from eBay, while Ryan made the trip to Spalding to return the moving van. The bed was simple to assemble. It consisted of only the frame, legs and multiple horizontal slats which were to be clipped in from the top. No screws were required because the weight of the person sleeping on the bed would, obviously, force the slats into the frame. Upon returning to London late at night, Ryan was surprised to see that Luke had done most of the unpacking and even assembled the bed. For the next few nights, the bed made concerning creaks and popping sounds, but Ryan simply passed this off as noises associated with a second-hand bed. Until one night, with an almighty thud, the bed gave way. As Ryan lay on the floor at 2 a.m., he could hear Luke chuckling uncontrollably in his bedroom. It emerged that Luke had assembled the bed upside down, somehow contorting the entire design into exactly the opposite orientation.

In many ways, experiences like these helped us break through the grief. They helped us move beyond our attempts to make sense of what had happened and presented the bare Sisyphean absurdity of our attempts to live.

However, as Albert Camus said, 'One must imagine Sisyphus happy.'[1] We learned to engage in life with a smile on our faces. Even if we had no idea what we were doing.

Skyline Stumble

RYAN

Dubai, April 2017. I admire the Burj Khalifa from the outside, standing an impressive 830m tall, with the illuminating sun reflecting from the glass exterior. My neck strains to see the very top as it pierces into the sky.

Now on the inside, the floor numbers flash in front of me as we effortlessly ascend above the skyline in the rocket-like lift.

One side of the building is surrounded by a lake of the purest blue water. From floor 148, the top observation deck, the view down looks as it did from the bottom, the lake of pure blue reflecting the sky above.

From this height the sunset is three minutes later than on the ground. With the fastest elevators in the world, covering the first 125 floors in a single minute, theoretically the day's sunset can be viewed twice.

I can view Dubai, 550m up, from the many balconies on the observation deck. They all have large, thick glass barriers on the edge, providing indescribable views across the city. One side of the building overlooks the lake with a view over the Persian Gulf. From another, the complex road network can be seen in full, sprawling across the city in a spaghetti-like arrangement. I take my place to soak up the views, pressing myself against the glass barriers.

I feel an uneasy urge; an urge that has arisen many times in the last year. I see the world differently now. There is a constant urge for a moment of release, for disconnectedness. At train stations I feel angst if I stand too close to the tracks and I fight a strange connection, a gravity, towards the path of passing trains.

Now, I fear that I'm fighting something invisible within. I can't tell if it is persuading me to step forward and finally put an end to my pain.

Here, atop the tallest building in the world, thoughts and visualisations about how I can climb over these large barriers are piercing through my consciousness.

These strange thoughts are like a virus spreading through my mind. Unconsciously, I find myself diverting my gaze downwards, looking for which side of the observation deck will allow me to avoid ledges along the way, enabling me to pick up the greatest speed before the ground comes rushing in as my saviour.

I'm certain I can scale the glass barriers; I have spent quite a large part of my youth scaling trees, lamp posts and scaffolding. At twenty-six, I am fitter and stronger than I was back then – getting over the barriers wouldn't be an issue.

I look around; nobody would be able to get to me in time if I made the scramble to get through these barriers.

Stop it! What am I thinking?

I pull myself back into the lobby and collapse on a sofa. I can't enjoy the view without these vivid thoughts. I don't want to die: at least that is what I keep telling myself. I realise my subconscious is trying to alert me: it isn't a desire I feel, so much as a warning. I leave because my thoughts are making me nauseous.

*

I am staying and studying in Abu Dhabi for three weeks on a work course, so I decide to make the trip to Atlantis hotel's Aquaventure Waterpark, situated on The Palm in Dubai. It is spread out over an impressive 170,000 square metres, with a 700-metre-long private beach; buggies continually travel the length of the park.

Even in this serene environment, I found it difficult to keep those unsettling thoughts from the Burj Khalifa from my mind.

Today, sunglasses on, lathered in sun cream, I am enjoying the meandering of the waves and the warmth of the sun on my skin. I am riding the 1.6km river rapids ride, which includes water escalators to enable me to repeat the loop without ever having to leave my rubber dinghy.

I could spend hours here simply letting my mind wander. I listen to what my mind is telling me as I repeat lap after lap. Perhaps the sunglasses will hide it; however, I'm pretty sure I am the first fully grown man the lifeguards have seen crying while floating around the rubber dinghy rapids. In fact, the faint tears are probably the only thing that reassures them I haven't died as my immobile body circles the route over and over again. I'm not sure how many people reach an emotional epiphany on the rubber dinghy rapids; however, I can't afford to be sentimental.

The course I came here for was in preparation for 'make-or-break' exams. I know I am capable of passing these exams as I have passed similar ones before; however, now I see that the foundations of my mind are much more fragile than I had appreciated. My future rests not on my academic ability and engineering competence, but on re-establishing my mental health and resilience.

My current state of mind offers me very little to be hopeful for.

An Open Question

RYAN

Visibly trembling, my eyes well up as I sit on the edge of my seat, tense and terrified. In the small waiting room, my eyes are focused a thousand yards through the wall. My mind is chaotic, my thoughts are incomprehensible. Every sound I hear, a door opening, someone's whispering voice, or a rustle of magazine, forces me into intense alertness.

I'm tuned to the noise of my name being called out. As my mind spins faster, the world spins slower. Time almost grinds to a halt as I wait.

Two weeks ago, Luke and I packed up and moved to a rental house in London, along with our two dogs, Indi and Bella.

The move was the first sense of progress I had felt in a year. The first twelve months had felt like Groundhog Day. We were living in the small rental house we had secured for Mum and Charlotte and we simply spent our time building up the most basic strength. Our days were filled with simple routine, carried out with the most exhausting but dogged determination.

Now I realise that I need to take advantage of this

momentum in my life and tackle what I had kept locked away. I need to dive deep into my pain if I want to get to its source and live free from its hold.

The wooden door creaks open.

'Ryan Hart?' The GP invites me in.

I take a seat, my hands are fidgeting as the nervousness boils over.

'How can I help you today?'

I look down to the floor. 'I would like to try antidepressants.'

My GP crooks her neck to look into my eyes. I notice her polite smile fade to concern.

'Can I ask what is wrong?'

I realise this is a question I've never been asked before. So simple, but one that reaches so deep.

I suddenly feel safe and my defences ease just a little, enough though for the emotional torrent to flood out. My body shakes with grief as I begin to purge the pain. I feel like a ball of yarn spinning loose.

The mask I've always worn has been shed and I feel an important moment has been reached. I will no longer pretend for anyone.

With my mind and body exhausted, I explain through a drained voice: 'My mum and little sister were murdered.'

My GP and I speak for close to an hour. I was terrified of this conversation, yet I shouldn't have been. This is the one I always wanted, the one I always needed, but I was taught by my father that it didn't exist.

This is the beginning of a new journey. This is the beginning of the unravelling of a life that my father had contorted and distorted. This is the beginning of living the life I had always intended to live with Mum and Charlotte by finding them inside of myself and removing any traces of my father.

A Leap of Faith

RYAN

I feel the steady, powerful pulsations of air beating at my chest. In comparison, I barely notice the faint fluttering of my racing heart.

My mouth is dry. This is it; there is no turning back. I shuffle closer to the edge and gaze down; I feel eyes following me, watching my every move. With a deep breath I look out towards the horizon and shout into the abyss; I need to feel strong if I'm going to jump.

It feels like my heart has stopped beating; the rush temporarily paralyses my mind and body. I let go of my desire for control and the wind moulds my body into position. I reach a physical and psychological equilibrium as I accelerate to 130mph. I have finally accepted the craving I have been fighting against for so long; I made the jump.

I have only forty-five seconds to enjoy the sensations and the art of human flight. I close my eyes to enjoy the final moments of freefall, take a deep breath and throw my hands behind me. I feel my body jolt and everything feels still. There is a moment of serene clarity as the roar of air turns to a faint breeze.

Now, I feel and hear my heart pounding in my chest. This time, my pounding heart makes me feel alive. This time, instead of looking down, I look up.

The pilot chute deployment had been successful, and I see the main parachute opened widely above me. In the distance I see the small plane as a speck in the sky.

Helmet unclipped, goggles peeled off and placed around my neck, I gather up my parachute and make my way back to the hangar.

Three weeks later, I collect a small booklet. I have just achieved my skydiving 'A' licence, after eighteen jumps.

The feeling that had terrified me, now exhilarates me. What I felt as fear, I now feel as power.

I own it.

Looking to the Horizon

It was through those moments of calamitous cooperation and entertaining incompetence that we both truly learned to live for each other. We have tried to create the open environment in which we can afford to make mistakes, the environment that our father denied us growing up.

Our convoluted convalescence has taught us that our blind spots to our suffering do not stop us projecting that suffering onto each other. Such logic, although it seemed to relieve our own distress initially, was about as intelligent as a child thinking they've disappeared because they've chosen to cover their own eyes. As a result, we've become much more open about what's on our minds, so we can resolve it immediately.

It is very possible that our adaptions saved our lives at the time of abuse. They were the solution to that previous problem. The difficulty for us now is in readapting our belief systems once more. As we've discovered, this often involves discarding parts of ourselves that we had become overly attached to and believed were 'us' but were instead defence mechanisms against our father. It is painful to wrench off our armour and leave our nakedness exposed to the world, but it also lightens our load. Our father's behaviour required us to continually learn from our struggles and reinvent ourselves based on our own intellectual discovery. It is this flexibility which provides us with the way out of the despair that he attempted to create.

Freedom comes from breaking the patterns of our behaviour established in an environment of abuse. It feels uncomfortable to do things that we have never done before; this is the deceptive safety that our habits appear to offer us.

In our past life, we often accepted the things that we felt we had no control over. We deluded ourselves into believing that we wanted the circumstances that were forced upon us. As children, we did not have the strength to change our circumstances and we needed to reduce our emotional distress. Where we had no control, we still demanded the impression of control. This was effective for survival, but we must be ready to move from this place now that we are safe.

Struggle makes things great. Struggle builds muscles,

struggle builds resistance and struggle builds understanding, compassion and connection. Yet, often in moments of difficulty we wished for a trivial and comfortable life. However, it was only in those moments of struggle, which we worried could break us, that we learned who we truly are. These are the moments we look back at which truly define us and force us to live a life we are fully engaged in.

Possibilities are often found in a world thrown upside down; now we realise that there are many options where before there seemed only one. It is disconcerting how uncertain and challenging freedom can feel but now we have found it, it's not something we will give up lightly.

To achieve true freedom, we have had to be honest about what we are truly afraid of. We have learned that if we don't process our emotions and let them out, they slowly diffuse and permeate throughout our beliefs. We may then adjust our beliefs in a maladaptive way to account for the huge emotional pressure within. If we were to allow this to happen then it may feel that the emotional torment has gone away, when in fact it has shifted our perspective so that we no longer see it.

In the past, we spent a huge amount of our energy on emotional regulation. This prevented ordinary emotional and social development because we were so restrictive with those parts of ourselves. We overcompensated and hid in our intellects. That became our escape from our emotional worlds. It is only now as we learn to overcome our emotional phobias that we become what lies behind the fear. The intellect that abstracted us from the world now gives in to a simple immersion in the world.

A life that we do not take control of is a life that is not lived. Whatever we had planned for this point in our life, it is now time for us to live. We cannot benefit from bitterness. We can only benefit from living. We are working hard to let the problems we face dissipate and not grow beyond the perspective that they truly deserve. After all, the ultimate revenge against cruelty is the refusal to imitate.

We do not feel lonely because we are aware of our mother's and Charlotte's presence within. Often every experience, no matter how dark, will have an angle from which it shines. We both know how incredibly lucky we were to have had Mum and Charlotte perform such important roles in our lives. In fact, we often reflect on what a shame it is for others who did not know them.

They taught us that the most important thing we can do is to live. Everything else is secondary. It is perhaps a sign of human arrogance to believe that we can understand everything, that everything can be understood, or that everything even needs to be understood. Life must be lived, not questioned. We cannot sit back and cynically ask the world to justify itself to us and answer for our suffering. Often our intellect is slow to perceive the things that we know in a greater sense. The world continues whether we comprehend it or not. That alone humbles our intellect and teaches us simply to live and not to always rely on understanding to guide us. When the world deals us hands that we cannot understand, we are learning to bend rather than forcing the world to break.

A powerful story about the ubiquity of suffering which highlights the importance of maintaining a correct perspective can be found in Buddhist literature. This is a story which has provided us both with strength and has helped us to understand that we are not the only ones who have suffered in this world. This perspective gives us a purpose and passion to help others who are in similar situations. The story goes like this:

> A young woman called Kisa Gotami sadly watched her son pass away when he was only a year old. She was overcome with grief. She begged everyone she met to help bring her son back to life, but to no avail. Eventually, someone suggested she visit the Buddha himself.
>
> The Buddha listened to her story and was very kind to her. He told her that he could help her if she could find five mustard seeds from a family who'd never experienced a death.
>
> Elated, Kisa Gotami set off to do just that, but having visited every home in her town she soon discovered that everyone at some point had known death or misfortune. She realised the lesson the Buddha had sought to teach her: suffering and death are a part of life that come to us all. At last, she was able to stop grieving the loss of her son and begin to live the rest of her life.

In the end, life is a Pyrrhic victory. Nature forever reminds us of how suddenly we may lose everything that we have built. As we are learning to accept this, we are beginning to live life on its own terms.

Every event in our lives is one that we must find a personal meaning for; a step to something greater. It's our responsibility to ensure that we are pleased with every effort that we have made in our lives. We must remember that we can always choose to create ourselves despite our circumstances, as our mother and Charlotte taught us. Even when we are bogged down in suffering, we refuse to forget the arc of our lives and what we wish to complete while we are here.

We have discovered that true life is not physical but reverberates in the things that we believe in and value. When we look outside of ourselves to try to understand our existence, we find coincidence and pseudo-causality; the locus of all things is inside each of us. No longer will we pretend that all the problems exist out in the world. Addressing our own problems will keep each of us busy for our lifetimes.

We have learned the hard way that life is not fair. Working hard will not always get us what we feel we deserve. It is up to us to be the arbiter, to take on the mantle of ensuring justice in our world. Compensation for our losses is never enough. It is clear that we must forgo self-pity because the only justice we can wish for is a life worth living.

We choose to be good not to get our dues but because we need to cultivate goodness in ourselves for our own sake. We internalise our goals and focus on strengthening our character so that we will always be rewarded for our work regardless of whether external success is bestowed upon us. Fundamentally, continuing to develop our character will increase our capacity for life.

Each of our encounters with evil reminds us of why we choose to be good. We are only victims the second we consider ourselves to be and a key reason we continue to survive is that we take our hardships face on and dedicate ourselves to the challenges we encounter. With each encounter we continue to build ourselves stronger. If we did not take responsibility for overcoming our suffering and waited on the world to remediate our situation, we would have collapsed under our burden. We have learned not to wait for the perfect world before participating honestly, otherwise we become part of the problem.

A key principle of our responsibility is that a good life doesn't happen to us; we must create it out of the bare materials we are given. It is not possible for us to feel guilt and shame with true responsibility. True responsibility doesn't lambast us pointlessly for the suffering our father has caused us; instead, it commits us to grow and improve with each event in our lives. We should only feel guilt and shame where we have failed in this task.

To give up and never persevere with our new lives is to assume that we have exhausted every possibility in life. Certainty is the forsaking of life itself; it is the absence of curiosity and curiosity is all that can sustain us in an imperfect world. Certainty is the deadening of the flow of nature and the human spirit; it is the slow murdering of meaning. Attachment to our experiences is as destructive as it is with our possessions. Our mother and sister would want us to engage in our new freedom from our father, with all of the uncertainty that freedom brings. We are beginning to let our past go and let our old hopes go. We are building new ones.

Fundamentally, what we look for we will inevitably

find. We mustn't spend our short lives looking for things that we don't want to find. What value is there in finding something worthless? We must now look for something beautiful. We will eventually find it and it will consume our lives. We must remember that our eyes only see where we choose to look, and we will never know what we're missing if we look in the wrong direction.

Casting a Light

Writing this book and finally reading it has provided us with a path that we didn't know was there until we had completed it. Writing is cathartic, but it also lays our internal contradictions bare and provides the ability to observe ourselves from a position of some objectivity. It is from here that we have been able to see our values in their cold, naked form. Writing is helping us to learn a new perspective.

It is gratifying to believe we are the centre of the universe, but this comes with an unhealthy narcissism which blows our sufferings out of all proportion and only punishes us. Therefore, we are learning to see ourselves in the correct proportion to the events in our lives; no bigger, no smaller.

As we wrote this book we felt many insights present themselves to us. It is almost as if we were learning by reading the elements of our subconscious laced between the lines of our own writing. As we explore our experiences, we continue to find fears cloaked in yet more fears; an exploration not dissimilar to unpacking a matryoshka doll. We have not reached the end of our self-exploration and we probably never will, but we have been on a voyage in a dark ocean and have found places within ourselves which provided us with refuge and self-compassion that we can always rely upon. We have learned to love ourselves and with that responsibility we must tear away any parts within which do not serve us and exist only to limit our possibilities.

We found that we were carrying heavy cargo and that if we wished to progress further we would have to leave behind what we no longer needed. Overcoming is not just a case of building strength; it is a case of becoming leaner too. Many aspects of us need to be sacrificed if we are to have a future at all.

We have not reached the goodness that our mother and sister guided us towards, but we are committed to that path. True commitment is often the hardest part. To leave on a perpetual journey means leaving behind a sense of security.

The comfort of waiting for others to save us from our circumstances will never achieve the safety we wish for. This comfort is only temporary and illusory, and when life breaches our false defences we will be weaker and less able to bear the storms. The only safety we can ever develop is in our capacity to endure what life has in store for us. The only people who can ever save us, in any circumstances, are ourselves.

Throughout the trauma of our experiences we have tried not to worry about our finite emotions in the face of our inevitable, infinite death. Emotions are simply the grounding force while we pursue larger causes. We can all find something that we think would make us happier but we all know something the loss of which would certainly make our lives worse. It is not pessimistic to focus on the loss of things we have, instead we let these reflections teach us gratitude. Despite what we have lost, we must learn to enjoy what we have without deprecating what we do not. Too often, an attempt at gratefulness becomes intolerance.

Our meaning is spreading the message of our mother's and Charlotte's unending love in the face of uncompromising evil. Hopefully our story will show how ordinary men can endure extraordinary circumstances with such brave examples to lead us. We hope that our story demonstrates that evil does not taint. Evil is not the inevitable consequence of misfortune and disadvantage. We must never feel picked on by fate or by humanity. They care little for us, certainly not enough to single us out.

We hope that telling our story will grasp the attention needed for honest and open public conversation. Those who are currently enduring domestic abuse need all of us to help them escape. To escape from domestic abuse, it is necessary for others, outside the abuse, to break through the false narratives.

Vulnerable women and children are not treated as heroes for standing up to their oppressors. There is no national day of mourning for those brave women and children killed for persistently choosing to love and live in a world that demanded hate. There is no recognition for those silently suffering but persevering bravely in the face of their dire circumstances.

But we think there should be.

*

The best of us do not survive in this brutal world. It is our job to ensure that they live on and to tell the message of their lives.

As a lighthouse shines into the darkness to guide weary travellers, our mother, Claire, and our sister, Charlotte, saved us.

We hope that their message can save others.

Flashback – Treasured Memories

RYAN

'What's going on, Ryan?' Charlotte laughs while fumbling around with the nine-piece jigsaw we had created.

Mum, Luke and I have bought Charlotte two tickets for Christmas to see Busted perform in the coming months. She has been talking about wanting to go but the tickets were all sold out. We'd planned well in advance and bought these months before.

The jigsaw is taking shape: a picture of the Busted members with some words spelling out the next clue.

'Look behind the TV?' Charlotte reads out curiously. 'OK then. Let's see what's behind the TV. . .', as a grin is developing across her face.

Charlotte gets up from the floor and shuffles to the TV, still wearing her PJs and slippers. I select Busted on my phone and the speakers begin playing 'What I Go to School For' as Charlotte picks up an envelope from behind the TV.

With the unopened envelope in her hand she screams, 'No you didn't! How did you get these?! I love you guys so much!' Charlotte tears open the envelope to reveal the tickets, with tears streaming down her face. She runs between Mum, Luke and me, hugging each of us and bouncing up and down.

Much of the afternoon is spent dancing to *Just Dance* on the Xbox as Charlotte shakes away the energy from her surprise.

'Let's go again!'

Just as we collapse in a heap on the sofa, Charlotte challenges us to another dance-off, seemingly with unlimited energy.

The dancing fills us with endless laughter. We jump around, bouncing off one another as we try to master the dance moves in the limited space we have. Bella joins in and jumps around with us as we dance the afternoon away, while Indi runs in excited circles around our feet.

'You're on camera!' our mum chuckles, as she attempts to catch our embarrassing moves on the new smartphone we had bought for her.

'I'm going to show this at your wedding, Charlotte. Your future husband needs to see this!' Mum jokes.

'Add it to the collection,' Charlotte replies, tears rolling down her face as she laughs at our attempts to haphazardly contort and twist ourselves to the music.

It's going to be difficult. It's going to be extremely difficult.
For many months or even years you won't be able to look

at photos without tears in your eyes, regretting the future which could have been. But a day will come when you will look upon those photos and be thankful for the good times you shared. You will smile at the treasured memories and remember them as vividly as if your mum and sister were still here.

    – Di, our family liaison officer

It's our second Christmas since the murders of Mum and Charlotte. Luke, Indi, Bella and I are all sat in the living room on Christmas morning. We reach into the pile of presents in the middle of the room, give it a squeeze and it lets out a loud squeak. Indi and Bella are both startled. They look inquisitively at us both; we nod and start shaking the present.

Excited, their tongues pop out and they both dive into the wrapped presents, grab them between their jaws and start shaking the wrapping paper off.

Balls, treats and squeaky chickens are now laid out across the floor among the shredded wrapping paper. Luke and I are in stitches watching them open each present and play with it for only a few seconds before diving in for the rest. We're eating our toast and they keep coming for rest breaks at our feet, pawing for a slice or two.

We remember when Charlotte taught them to open their own presents and how it made us all laugh, and we've never stopped since. As we sit back while Indi and Bella play with each other, we look up at the photos of Mum and Charlotte which line the living room, and see one in particular from their last Christmas.

We both realise that the memories they gave us will always be with us and that these moments are the ones we need to cherish above all others.

Every time we hear the songs from that Christmas, a smile finds its way to our faces. We will remember Charlotte jumping on our backs as part of the dance routine, our dogs frantically trying to get involved in the fun, and our mum's smile as she watched us make fools of ourselves. We didn't know it then, but it was to be our last Christmas together.

Our father tried to take everything from us. But he can never take these treasured memories.

DOMESTIC ABUSE
SUPPORT

The Serious Crime Act 2015 created a new offence of controlling or coercive behaviour in intimate or familial relationships. The offence carries a maximum sentence of five years' imprisonment, a fine or both.

The law defines the terms as the following:

- Controlling behaviour: a range of acts designed to make a person subordinate and/or dependent by isolating them from sources of support, exploiting their resources and capacities for personal gain, depriving them of the means needed for independence, resistance and escape and regulating their everyday behaviour.
- Coercive behaviour: a continuing act or a pattern of acts of assault, threats, humiliation and intimidation or other abuse that is used to harm, punish, or frighten their victim.

Evidence which could assist the police in prosecuting coercive behaviour includes:

- Text messages, emails or voicemail recordings
- Photographs
- Medical records
- Bank statements
- Diaries documenting:
  - Dates friends and family were last seen
  - Dates hobbies had to be cancelled
  - Dates employment had to be ended
  - Any false allegations made by the abuser to threaten you

If you ever feel in danger, call 999 immediately. The 24-hour National Domestic Violence Freephone Helpline 0808 2000 247 is a partnership between Women's Aid and Refuge, and offers confidential support, advice and help. If you have any uncertainties at all about your partner's behaviour, please call to check. Coercive control goes under the radar of services precisely because many victims feel embarrassed recalling incidents where they haven't been physically assaulted. Let those who understand this crime make that decision. Remember that a manipulator might seem nice at the start of a relationship; their aim is to trick a victim into dependence and then begin the ratcheting away of freedoms.

Our goal would be achieved if we can encourage women (and those around them) to regularly check the behaviours of their partners in the same way that we regularly check our physical health. Coercive control is a malignant form of relationship and should be treated so. As with most diseases, catch it early! Do not allow an abuser to rationalise their manipulation of you, or for the condition to metasta-sise. As with cancer, it seems that many in coercive control relationships misinterpret their conditions for more benign circumstances. Let's be frank, if men and women can honestly talk about checking their own testicles and breasts in casual conversation, then why are we still embarrassed to check if our partner's behaviour is manipulative? It could save your life.

If you need to escape urgently, Women's Aid and Refuge both run refuge services to look after women and children who have had to flee their homes.

Finally, our candid advice: if you start to get a bad feel-ing early in a relationship that tells you there is something wrong, get out! There are lots of kind men who are not abusive, and no relationship is worth the sacrifices that coercive control demands. If you ever think: *It's not that bad, I'm not being hit*, this should be a warning sign, not reassurance.

Abusers will never change. Do not waste your energy or hope believing that they will. They are skilled manipula-tors and will lead you down a very long road of false hope. Inevitably, you will become exhausted, alone, without resources and they will have embedded their manipulation within your mind through the aggregation of those 'it's not that bad' incidents. Remember that coercive control is the most accurate predictor of fatality. Do not interpret a lack of violence to mean that you are safe.

It could well mean the opposite.

HOW TO SPOT DOMESTIC ABUSE

Throughout this book, we have been describing abusers as 'he' and their victims as female or children. It should be noted that women are disproportionately victims of abuse, and men are disproportionally the perpetrators. There are specific structural characteristics unique to how men are treated as perpetrators and women are treated as victims which is what we have attempted to highlight in this book.

There are also key beliefs that indicate a risk of perpetration: misogynistic, outdated gender roles backed up by a media-reinforced patriarchal entitlement.

Our experience has clearly shown us that domestic abuse is a male criminal issue and female health issue. Not the other way around. Consistent patterns of male violence certainly shouldn't be dismissed as if women were aggressors provoking male 'mental health issues'. It appears that the perpetrator has cast himself as the perfect victim to the public. We hope we can go some way to remediate this lie.

As our story shows, we cannot rely on victims of abuse to identify and tackle their situation alone. We cannot simply ask someone if their father, partner or relative is abusive. The answer will almost always certainly be 'no'. This may stem from fear, guilt, shame or the fact that the victim is completely unaware that they are living in an abusive relationship. Hopefully you can understand this dynamic slightly more having read our story. An outside perspective is needed to break through the false narratives that the victim has been fed and help them identify their situation for what it is.

Our father would often tell our mother she was 'lucky as most men would beat their wives' for what she had done – buying a £3 coffee from her own wages without first consulting our father, for example. She was told that the hours, and sometimes days, of his shouting, belittling and criticising were an act of compassion and generosity because he was duly entitled to physically assault her for her disobedience. A victim of abuse may feel that they are to blame for the abuse they receive, as they struggle to conform to ever-changing arbitrary rules set by their abuser.

For children especially, open questions need to be asked, such as: 'Tell me about the rules in your household' or 'What happens if you break the rules?' Again, for a child who has only lived in an environment of domestic abuse, the arbitrary rules to which they are held accountable may not seem out of the ordinary, and so they may not feel it necessary to even point them out. A more revealing insight may be obtained by asking more specific questions like: 'What happens if you accidentally drop a plate and it breaks?' or 'What happens if you are late home from school?'

Victims of abuse have their social and support networks severed. Often, the only times a victim is away from their abuser is at work, during a visit to the GP or to use public toilets, if they are allowed out of the house. It is key that these places take on board their incumbent responsibility to raise awareness of domestic abuse and coercive control for women and point them in the direction of services. We all have the responsibility to decrease stigma by talking about domestic abuse.

We should all be able to recognise the subtle signs that a colleague or friend may be in a coercive and controlling relationship. Hopefully by now you have an insight into the lives of victims of abuse and the mindset of an abuser.

Remember that the National Domestic Violence Helpline is there for concerned relatives and friends as a valuable first port of call to discuss fears, too. Intervening without careful thought may be dangerous to you and potentially put the person who you are concerned about in more danger.

Below are just a few signs that you may notice in a friend or colleague. Don't ignore them!

- Not going anywhere outside of work without their partner being present.
- Not able to suddenly change their routine as everything needs to be as per an agreed routine with their partner.
- Decreasing social life outside of the home; less contact via social media, text messages or email. Decreasing time spent on hobbies and meeting up with friends.

- Their partner contacting the place of work and asking if the victim is there. He will most likely have a trivial excuse for making the call, asking her which petrol station he should fill up at, for example. The reason for the call is to keep track of her to ensure that she is where he expects her to be. Abusers are paranoid whenever their victim is out of their sight.
- Their partner turning up at the place of work or place of recreation/sport/hobby unannounced.
- Their partner ringing your number (as they are going through the victim's phone to see who she has been contacting) or replying on behalf of the victim.

Domestic abuse needs each and every one of us to have the courage to call out immoral behaviours, to challenge the false narratives and victim-blaming and to make a stand against tyranny behind closed doors. Every woman and child deserves to live free from fear and violence. We all have a responsibility to act to allow them to achieve this basic human right.

ENDNOTES

Preface

1. Bartlett, K. T., Rhode, D. L. & Grossman, J. L., *Gender and Law: Theory, Doctrine, Commentary 6th edition.* (Aspen Publishers, 2013).
2. Rennison, C. M. & Welchans, S., 'Special Report: Intimate Partner Violence', Bureau of Justice Statistics (accessed January 2019).
3. Russell P. Dobash, R. Emerson Dobash, *When Men Murder Women.* (Oxford University Press, 2015).
4. Dobash et al., *When Men Murder Women.*
5. Office for National Statistics, 'Homicide in England and Wales: Year Ending March 2017', www.ons.gov.uk (accessed September 2018).
6. Adams, D., *Why Do They Kill?: Men Who Murder Their Intimate Partners.* (Nashville: Vanderbile University Press, 2007).
7. Adams, D., *Why Do They Kill?.*
8. Taylow, S., G. Schmutte, K. Leonard & J. Cranston,

'The effects of alcohol and extreme provocation on the noxious electric shock', *Motivation and Emotion*, Vol. 3, pp. 73–81. (1979).

9. Halket, M. M., Gormley, K., Mello, N., Rosenthal, L. & Mirkin, M. P., 'Stay with or Leave the Abuser? The Effects of Domestic Violence Victim's Decision on Attributions Made by Young Adults', *Journal of Family Violence,* Vol. 29. (2013).

10. Office for National Statistics, 'Homicide in England and Wales'.

11. Halket et al., 'Stay with or Leave the Abuser?'.

12. Domestic Abuse Interventions Programs, 'Violence Wheel', www.theduluthmodel.org (accessed September 2018).

13. Boundless, 'Spousal Abuse'. (Boston, Massachusetts, 2015).

14. Campbell, J. C., 'Commentary on Websdale: lethality assessment approaches: reflections on their use and ways forward', *Violence Against Women*, Vol. 11. (2005).

15. Home Office, https://assets.publishing.service. gov.uk/government/uploads/system/uploads/ attachment_data/file/482528/Controlling_or_coercive_behaviour_-_statutory_guidance.pdf

16. Caldwell, J. E., Swan, S. C., Woodbrown, V. D., 'Gender differences in intimate partner violence outcomes', *Psychology of Violence*, Vol. 2. (2012).

17. Swan, S. C., Gambone, L. J., Caldwell, J. E., Sullivan, T. P. & Snow, D. L., 'A Review of Research on Women's Use of Violence With Male Intimate Partners', www.

ncbi.nlm.nih.gov (accessed September 2018).

18. Stark, E., *Coercive Control*. (New York: Oxford University Press, 2009).

19. United Nations Office on Drugs and Crime, 'Global Study on Homicide', www.unodc.org (accessed September 2018).

20. Arendt, H., *Eichmann in Jerusalem*. (New York: The Viking Press, 2006).

21. Strong, B., DeVault, C. & Cohen, T., *The Marriage and Family Experience: Intimate Relationships in a Changing Society*. (Boston: Cengage Learning, 2010).

1. In the Dark

1. Stark, E., *Coercive Control*. (New York: Oxford University Press, 2009).

2. Everytown for Gun Safety, 'Mass Shootings in the United States: 2009–2016', www.everytownresearch. org (accessed April 2017).

3. The Home Office, 'The economic and social costs of domestic abuse', www.gov.uk (accessed January 2019).

4. Rand Corporation, 'The cost of terrorism in Europe', www.rand.org (accessed June 2018).

5. HM Treasury, 'Spending review and autumn statement 2015', www.gov.uk (accessed June 2018).

6. Women's Aid, 'The Femicide Census', www.womens-aid.org.uk (accessed January 2019).

7. GTD, 'Global Terrorism Database', www.start.umd. edu (accessed January 2019).

8. From Martin Luther King, Jr.'s 'Letter from Birmingham Jail', Stanford, California, 1963 (pdf). The Martin Luther King, Jr., Research and Education Institute (retrieved 12 October, 2017).

3. Myths of Abuse

1. Office for National Statistics, 'Focus on Violent Crime and Sexual Offences Compendium', www.ons.gov.uk (accessed June 2018).

2. S. Walby & J. Allen, *Domestic Violence, Sexual Assault and Stalking: Findings from the British Crime Survey* (London, 2004).

3. Office for National Statistics, 'Homicide in England and Wales: Year Ending March 2017', www.ons.gov.uk (accessed June 2018).

4. Samaritans, Suicide statistics report, https://www.samaritans.org/about-samaritans/research-policy/suicide-facts-and-figures (accessed January 2019).

5. A. Howerton et al, 'Understanding Help Seeking Behaviour Among Male Offenders: Qualitative Interview Study', *BMJ* (London, 2007) 334:303.

6. C. Emslie et al, 'Men's Accounts of Depression: Reconstructing or Resisting Hegemonic Masculinity?', *Social Science & Medicine* (London, 2005), 62 (9) pp. 2246–57.

7. H. Sherwood, 'Violence Between Individuals "Kills Nine Times More People" Than Wars', www.theguardian.com (accessed May 2017).

8. Office for National Statistics, 'Focus on Violent Crime

and Sexual Offence: Year Ending March 2015', www.ons.gov.uk (accessed June 2018).

9. Ministry of Defence, 'British fatalities: Operations in Iraq', www.gov.uk (accessed May 2017).

10. Ministry of Defence, 'Operations in Afghanistan', www.gov.uk (accessed May 2017).

11. H. Pidd, 'Men Killed 900 Women in Six Years in England and Wales, Figures Show', www.theguardian.com (accessed May 2017).

12. H. Sherwood, 'Violence Between Individuals . . .', www.theguardian.com (accessed May 2017).

13. J. Kasperkevic, 'Private Violence: Up to 75% of Abused Women Who Are Murdered Are Killed After They Leave Their Partners', www.theguardian.com (accessed May 2017).

4. Overcoming

1. B. Spinoza, *Ethics*. (London, 1996).

2. V. E. Frankl, *Man's Search for Meaning: The classic tribute to hope from the Holocaust*. (London, 2004).

5. Our Meaning

1. F. Nietzsche, *Twilight of the Idols*. (Oxford, 1998).

2. V. E. Frankl, *Man's Search for Meaning: The classic tribute to hope from the Holocaust*. (London, 2004).

6. Our Light

1. A. Camus, *The Myth of Sisyphus*. (London, 2005).

ACKNOWLEDGEMENTS

There are too many people to thank. A hand has been extended everywhere we turned, reaching from those with whom we have shared decades together, through to total strangers.

Throughout our meandering convalescence we have found many new and unexpected friends who have artfully and gently brought us back into the world and helped us begin to trust again. Each step of our journey leads us to learn more about ourselves as we throw off our chains and begin to explore our new freedom; a freedom we never knew that we lacked.

As slow as our recovery may look, inside our lives are progressing fast. Each moment upturns our old lives and we find ourselves moving in new directions as we push our once-confined boundaries vastly outwards.

We have not had time to thank everyone throughout the last two years as we have been so consumed with rebuilding ourselves. However, we hope that you all recognise the positive impact you have had on us. Each moment of degradation we have suffered throughout our lives is grad-ually built back up with each moment of compassion.

Our mother held very fond memories of her time at work and always spoke admiringly of all her colleagues. There are too many to mention, but we would like to particularly thank Dale, Laraine, Dean and Sue. Not only for the happi-ness you brought our mother, but also for the support you gave us over the past two years.

To Louise and Kelly, we doubt we would have navigated the first days, weeks and months in our dissociated daze had it not been for your care.

Thank you, Mike Jackson, and all of Ryan's colleagues in Reading. In what was a challenging time for Ryan lead-ing up to the attack, unbeknown to all, a supportive and friendly work environment made all the difference. Thank you, Mike, for your immediate reaction to the tragedy and doing everything you could to help us; you are a distin-guished example of the kind of man the world needs more of.

Thank you to our family liaison officers, Di and Debs, who worked tirelessly in the aftermath of the attack to guide us through those difficult days with such compas-sionate support.

We owe a great deal to a long-time family friend, Kate Haynes, for the friendship you gave our mother and the unyielding love and concern for us in the aftermath of our tragedy.

We are grateful to the community of Spalding, particu-larly the staff at the Castle Sports Complex who rushed to the aid of our mother and sister, and to Cheryl for easing us into the gym and encouraging us back into exercise and yoga. We must thank Abigail, Nikki and all the dog walkers for being our supports, whether you knew or not, when we were most vulnerable.

We were humbled by Spalding High School, Morrisons and Wood Green, The Animals Charity for the opportunity to leave lasting memorials to our mother and sister. We are honoured that you wished to share in recognising their contributions to our lives and the lives of those whom they touched.

We would like to thank Refuge and Women's Aid for reaching out to us and giving us the encouragement and support to initially share our story. The Walk4 event, with so many other inspirational domestic abuse survivors and inspiring campaigners, was influential in our journey to commit to act on domestic abuse.

Thank you to Rossalyn for helping us to tell our story with the *Guardian* and helping to articulate coercive control so eloquently.

Thank you to everyone who provided us with kind company while we were at our most wounded: Adam, Nick, Tristram and Jason, Jess, Adam and Claire and our extended family.

Luke would like to thank those who have given him the space to begin working again in a positive and encouraging environment, particularly Shona, Finlay, Lindsey and Bob.

Surrey police and ESDAS have been so important in building our confidence back, especially Debbie, Michelle, Bridie, Lisa, Juliet, Bex and Charlotte. Their infectious energy and passion have motivated us to continue speaking out about domestic abuse. Telling our story with the agencies in Surrey has not only been cathartic, but has helped us make wonderful new friendships. We did not know at the time, but those speeches sowed the seeds of this book.

Thank you to all of those we continue to meet who are so active in fighting against domestic abuse and have helped mentor us in this new world, particularly Frank Mullane. We continue to be overwhelmed with admiration at the motivation, passion and relentless determination for good that we see within this community.

Ryan would like to particularly thank Ruth Aitken for her inspiration, care and selflessness. Thank you for your generous time and help; Ryan's recovery, this book, and everything good which comes from it, would not have been possible without you.

A huge thank you to Ben. The times that you and Charlotte were together were the happiest of her life. Your relationship filled our mother with joy.

Finally, our mother, Claire, and little sister, Charlotte. This book, and all the work we do to fight against domestic abuse, is your legacy. We will continue to resist evil and aspire to live in your image. You were, and always will be, our role models and inspiration.

ABOUT THE AUTHORS

Luke and Ryan Hart can be contacted via Twitter @CoCoAwareness, Facebook @LukeandRyanHart or through their website: www.CoCoAwareness.co.uk.

They both speak frequently at events and deliver training on coercive control, domestic abuse and resilience. So far, they have trained police officers, police community support officers, NHS personnel and legal professionals in the Crown Prosecution Service as well as engaging with children and young people. They are White Ribbon Ambassadors and Refuge Champions and regularly speak out against male violence towards women and children, as well as working with other charities such as Women's Aid and the NSPCC.